MY JOURNEY OF LIFE WITH PTSD

Daniel Osborne

AuthorHouse™ UK
1663 Liberty Drive
Bloomington, IN 47403 USA
www.authorhouse.co.uk
UK TFN: 0800 0148641 (Toll Free inside the UK)
UK Local: 02036 956322 (+44 20 3695 6322 from outside the UK)

Because of the dynamic nature of the Internet, any web addresses or links contained in this book may have changed
since publication and may no longer be valid. The views expressed in this work are solely those of the author and do
not necessarily reflect the views of the publisher, and the publisher hereby disclaims any responsibility for them.

Any people depicted in stock imagery provided by Getty Images are models,
and such images are being used for illustrative purposes only.
Certain stock imagery © Getty Images.

This book is printed on acid-free paper.

ISBN: 978-1-6655-8994-9 (sc)
ISBN: 978-1-6655-8993-2 (e)

Print information available on the last page.

Published by AuthorHousen 07/07/2021

author HOUSE®

CONTENTS

ACKNOWLEDGEMENTS

I am dedicating this in loving memory of my late mother Freya Osborne and father Ronnie Osborne as well as my aunt Meredith also my best friend Stan the man RIP. I miss you all so much; my life is not the same without you all in it. I hope that you are looking down on me and are proud of the son that you have made me into.

Also, I would like to thank my wonderful daughter, Gabrielle Osborne, for always being there for me and helping through so many difficult things. You have been truly amazing in all that you do for me. You helped me when we both lost so much. I couldn't wish to have a more wonderful loving, caring daughter. I am so proud of the woman that you have become and am honoured to be your father.

I also wish to thank Dr Janice for all the help she showed me over the years. She helped me seek the correct help that I needed. She never gave up hope in me. I thank you from the bottom of my heart. You have been such a tower of strength in all that you have done for my family and me. You will never be forgotten. Without your continued help and support with all I have gone through, I don't know where I would be today. If you ever moved to another surgery, I would have to follow, as you are the only doctor I would see.

I would like to take this point to thank Damian from Talk Time. You helped me face a few demons, and my sessions with you were most helpful in helping me have a better understanding of the traumas we talked about in our sessions. I wish you all the best for your future and wish we could have continued our sessions to the end.

I would also like to thank three people who have stood by me through thick and thin. James, we have been mates for as long as I can remember. We have helped each other through all sorts of difficulties since we have known each other, far too many to remember or list. We had our ups and downs, but you have never treated me the way others have, those who threw my friendship away. Thank you for being a good mate. I would also like to thank your two brothers, whom have also been good mates who have stood by me and not thrown my friendship back in my face.

Finally, I would like to say a massive thank you to Dr Williamson. You have given me strength and courage and pushed me all the way to become the person I now look at in the mirror each morning. I have talked with you about all my fears and traumas that I have suffered with for so long in my life. You helped me get a sense of direction in my life and enabled me to find a pathway to finding that old me that I once was. You must take a lot of credit for the way I am approaching the traumas that we talked about for so many months. You pushed me to tell you exactly what was going through my mind. If you had not, I would not have a clearer respect and understanding for what I have suffered alone with for so long.

I feel I am slowly becoming the one who is waiting for me at the top of my greasy ladder You have helped me leave the old battered, traumatised, shattered, exhausted, and mentally scarred one with PTSD at the bottom of the ladder, never again to step foot on each of its greasy rungs. It's a difficult journey to the top.

So hopefully I can say a final goodbye to the old traumatised Daniel Osborne and welcome the new and more confident replacement, the positive and less traumatised Daniel Osborne.

I would to also thank each and every member of staff from Authourhouse who have stood by me from start to finish and backed me 100% in finally getting this manuscript published each and everyone from each process from the initial phone call I made then to the evaluation team, and also the editorial team and then on to the final team in the design and print and publication you have all encouraged me from the beginning and have spoken highly that this was a worthy project you were all happy to back me with so from the bottom of my heart I thank each of you for all your support.

INTRODUCTION TO MY LIFE WITH PSTD

My name is Daniel Osborne and I was born in my parent's bedroom in 1968 in the united kingdom where I have lived in the UK all of my life I have a beautiful daughter who is grown up and married and has 4 children of her own and I also have a son who is grown up also and has just had his first child with his partner so I am a granddad to 5 amazing boys.

My life is currently in an amazing place and I could not ask for more but in order for my life to get where it is today I had to take a journey that took me to the darkest place on earth where I felt like my life was pushed into the bottom of a dark well with a ladder against the wall of the inside of the well but as you will read through this book and my journey you will understand the difficulties that laid ahead of me to get out of this dark wishing well and try and reclaim the lost happy me that was awaiting to be rediscovered before I was lost and alone in the wishing well with only my own thoughts for comfort so welcome on board to my journey of life.

A life with PTSD (posttraumatic stress disorder) is a life of being trapped in a horrific nightmare, a dream state of mind, a life of constant nightmares and flashbacks that are filled with your worst innermost haunting traumas, and images of things that are unexplainable to most people (friends, family, and loved ones) who cannot share or help you. As a sufferer of PTSD for over 20 years, I found myself writing this book to help enable myself to read and look back on it in later years and reflect on how life really is with having PTSD.

Coming to terms and accepting that you are a sufferer with PTSD is something that you are never prepared for or could have ever imagined happening to yourself or a loved one. PTSD can take a long time to show itself and for you to start making any sort of sense as to what is going on. You may find yourself breaking down in public places, having intrusive flashbacks that feel so real and so realistic to the trauma or traumas of what you have witnessed or have gone through that to begin to make sense of it all will take a very long time indeed.

I am writing this book of my personal battle with PTSD to help myself understand what I have had to live with on my own, with no family support other than my daughter, and how it has in some ways destroyed the old me and made me into the person that I have become today, twenty years on. I write with an understanding of what I now know of my own experience's with PTSD and to try to help someone who maybe suffering with PTSD or a similar problem, or to try and help a loved one or family member help with picking up and noticing the signs that may help them relate to someone they love or care for and help give them an understanding of what may be going on with a loved one and what they can do to try and help.

There are many ways to get help and support with what you are going through. The main thing that I would strongly state straight away is that you are not alone. Make yourself aware that you are suffering with some life-changing things that you have never suffered with before your traumatic event/events that you have put to one side. It's normal. It will pass given the time; after all, I survived my traumas and am still here, still alive and living my life.

Take time out and look at what is actually going on in your mind in your daily routines of life. Is this reminder, this flashback, or image of your trauma so vivid that it's like reliving the same trauma or nightmare over and over again each day, to the point of becoming your very own Groundhog Day?

To begin to give you an understanding of my experiences with PTSD, I have to go back a bit further into my own past and show you how it affected my life in severe ways, not to mention all the complications that it caused me to go through and suffer with alone, with only the love and support of my daughter. I will go further back into my life to an early stage of understanding things as we progress further into this book.

To start with my own experience and difficulties, I am only going back in time to roughly 20 years ago, when things began to start getting difficult for me. The year was 2000, and my life started to get difficult due to an injury I sustained during my time working for a friend doing block paving and cement driveways. After doing this job for a few years, I started to get severe back pain and leg pain on the left side of my body.

Over the course of the next month or so, the pain got so severe that it prevented me from working, so I went to see my doctor I have been registered with for many years, a lovely woman by the name of Dr Janice, at my local surgery. I explained the difficulties I was having in walking, sitting down, and getting in a bath, in addition to the difficulties I had trying to get in and out of bed and the discomfort of sleeping. The agony that I felt was unbearable.

She helped me lie down on a couch and gave my spine a thorough examination as she checked for damage. I could feel the spasms in the lower part of my spine. She checked the reflexes in my left leg and foot, which was agony. After she did so, she then helped me up from the couch and aided me in sitting upright in the chair. 'Well, I have some bad news for you,' she said.

'What is it? What's causing me so much pain?' I asked her.

'After examining your spine, I think that you have two compressed vertebrae in your lower spine, which has trapped and is crushing the main nerve in your body, the sciatic nerve, which links to all your muscles in the body.'

'What are the long-term effects of it? What has to be done to stop it?' I asked.

Dr Janice told me she was going to refer me to hospital to have an MRI scan done to find out the full extent of the damage to the nerve and spine.

'How long is that going to take?' I asked.

'I will try to get an appointment pushed through as quickly as possible. I know you live on your own and that you do a lot for your elderly parents.'

I'd walk or drive to my parents' twice a day every day, as my mam was bad on her legs now and didn't go down the street anymore. She couldn't get the daily papers or buy her cigarettes. So I'd go up every day to do it for her and to see if they needed anything else done, whether it was shopping or housework.

As the months dragged by and the pain in my lower back and left leg got worse each day, it now took me over an hour to walk to my parents', which would normally take me ten minutes when healthy.

I had lost the ability to drive a car due to the severity of the pain. I had almost become completely disabled in my left leg and needed the aid of crutches to enable me to walk to my parents to do their shopping and such things. My condition continued to get worse every day, and I was forever going backwards and forwards to see my doctor. She tried lots of different tablets for the pain, but she did warn me that none would relieve much of the pain and the only way to do that would be to find out the extent of the damage I had caused after I had an MRI scan, which she was still pushing to get it sorted out as quickly as possible.

I suffered twelve months or more of sheer torture and pain, dragging my disabled leg up and down to my parents' to see to their daily needs. My parents knew how difficult it was for me to walk there and would always say, 'Don't keep coming up every day; you can hardly stand straight, let alone keep walking here every day.'

'Who is going to come get you your papers and go for your cigarettes and other things if not me? You have no one else to do it for you.' I would tell my mother not to worry about me, that I would be going in hospital soon and have surgery on my spine. The doctors had assured me that after I had it, I would be near enough back to normal and free of pain.

It was the longest twelve months of my life with the constant pain and daily suffering that I had to cope with. But I had the surgery after the long twelve months of waiting and forever going to my doctor for tablets to relieve the pain and muscle spasms in the left side of my body. Although now 20 years on after the surgery, I still suffer with nerve damage in my left leg and also lots of muscle spasms and discomfort in my lower spine.

That was just the start of my problems and only a small piece of the difficulties that I was to face only a year or so after my operation! The next section leads up to how difficult my life would become and the first real trauma that I was to encounter. It started when I was out one evening with a group of friends, having a few social drinks and playing a game of pool. I recall that I had taken my jacket off, leaving my mobile phone in a pocket, and placed it on the back of the chair. As the night went on, we decided to leave this pub and get a taxi back to where we normally drink.

While in the taxi, I checked my phone and saw that I had about twenty missed calls from my mother and father. Looking at my phone, I knew something was not right. I immediately rang back, and my brother, whom I will get to later in the book, answered the phone, telling me they had been ringing me all night to inform me that my mother had had a fall in the family home and an ambulance was on its way.

I immediately directed the taxi to my parents' house, as I was close by. That was the day things began to fall apart for me. Upon arriving at my parents', my so-called brother and my loving father had a right go at me about my not answering my mobile phone. Now please learn this lesson, as it is something that has stuck with me from that evening onwards: always have your phone with you at all times and never switch it off or put it on silent. I learnt about their frustration at not being able to reach me, although my phone was on and not silenced; I just never heard it above the noise of a crowded pub.

After their initial shouting, my attention was directed straight to my wonderful mother, who was about seventy-two or seventy-three at the time. She was in severe pain after her fall. I comforted her until the ambulance arrived to tend to her. She was taken to our local hospital, which is where I had undergone surgery on my spine years earlier. I followed the ambulance in a taxi, and my father went with my brother in his car. They took my mother into the A&E ward, and I followed them. She was taken into a cubicle, were she was examined and then taken for X-rays. After a few hours of waiting, we were given the bad news that she had broken her leg and pelvis in several places and that she needed surgery. From this moment in time, things in my life would get far worse than I could ever have imagined.

After my mother had undergone her surgery, I then had to start the process of its future long-term complications and how it was to change the course of my life forever. My poor mother (God bless her) now had to spend months in hospital, which I visited every day, sometimes twice a day, as I took my father to see my mother and to support him. My mother and father had never been away from each other overnight in over fifty years, so the strains were beginning to show on my elderly father at an early stage. After a few months, our concerns for my mother became more and more worrying.

During daily visits as we sat comforting my mother, we got concerned about things such as the way she began to speak; she said things that at the time we put down to medication. She would say she had just finished work, or that she had been down the street, or that people had been to see her in hospital when they had not been. My father was getting very upset and confused about why she was not able to go to the family home where I was born in the upstairs bedroom in October 1968.

All my father wanted was his beloved wife home so he could look after her. He used to go on about this each day. I'd say, 'Mam will be home soon, Dad. She needs time for things to heal properly after her operations.' This would reassure him slightly. Deep down I had begun to prepare myself for what I was about to have thrust upon me after I had a private meeting with my mother's doctor at the hospital, where I expressed my concerns about my mother and the length of time it had been since she'd been admitted. She was unable to walk, and then there was the way she was speaking. I recall this as if it were yesterday.

My mother was unable to return to the family home, as she would need full-time carers to look after her and to change her, to see to all of her needs, to dress her, feed her, put her to bed, take her to the toilet, and so on. My life had been altered forever in that room; my soul and heart had had pieces torn from them from the instant heartbreak, and the feeling will live with me forever.

The doctor explained that my mother was now suffering with dementia and that the hospital could do no more for her. They wanted to arrange to have my mother put into a care home to be looked after.

My heart filled with sorrow and complete heartache when I heard this. I was now on my own. I had to somehow find the words to explain to my elderly father that after over fifty years of sharing his life with my mother, this was now to end and she would have to go into care.

This is where things truly began to fall apart for me. How would I find the words, strength, or courage to explain to a frail 76-year-old dad that his wife, my mam, wouldn't be coming home and was going to need full-time care?

The words were somehow found, the explanations were said, and my heart was totally broken and torn apart. I was the youngest of five children and was left with this to cope with, with no help other than the truly remarkable support of my young daughter and also the support of a wonderful friend named Sabrina.

At the time of my mother being admitted to her first care home, I was also trying to juggle my working life as a painter and decorator living single in a two-bedroom home while trying to bring my daughter up. It soon became apparent to me that this was also going to change. I had undergone training for a more highly paid career as an asbestos operative and started to work away from home, which was a severe strain, as it meant having to leave my elderly father on his own in the family home, coping without Mam being there. But it became manageable for a while, until I got my friends at the time as well as myself excellent jobs at a power station in Cumbria, which we were all looking forward to. We could all earn a decent wage, and I could travel home to take my father to see my mother, as she had now been moved to a new nursing home only about a mile away from his home.

Before I started working in Cumbria with my friends, I was with my father, taking him to see my mother at the nursing home, and that's when the next journey of despair and testing times was about to begin. I observed the difficulties and obstacles that were now becoming more apparent and ever so more concerning to me. My father's frailty and health was becoming a major concern. I suddenly realised that he was not coping well and not looking after himself. I had a talk with him while we were visiting my mother at the care home about the job I was preparing to start, about how often I would be home (every weekend), and about his ability to go to the care home daily to see his wife. I wanted to try to keep things as normal as possible.

So after a long talk and much deliberating, I started my new job in Cumbria. After the third or fourth day of inductions and training, my mind couldn't settle because of the concerns about my father. After talking with my friends and listening to their advice, I found myself doing something that I had promised myself all my life I would not do: phone the only sibling I sort of spoke with.

I asked him to do one simple thing: phone social services and ask them for an assessment to be implemented for some home help on a daily basis for my father. It was not an unfair request to make, as everything else had been left to me to do. This response I was given floored me.

'Hi, it's your brother Daniel. I'm ringing you to ask if you could do me a favour. I have just started a new job in Cumbria and will be home each weekend to see to Dad and take him for his shopping, to see Mam at the nursing home, and to see to our auntie [my father's sister, aged 90 years]. I'm phoning to see if you could phone social services and organise some home help for Dad, as I am concerned about him living on his own and being bad on his legs, not to mention his overall health.'

The response from my brother went as follows. 'I am sorry, but I don't have time to do that. I have a family of my own to look after and see to. Father will be OK going to the nursing home by taxi.' Take into account that this so-called loving son, as he liked to portray himself, lived fairly local and drove to pick his two sons up weekly to see them, passing our father's on his journey. He would never stop by to see my father other than when he used to get his Viagra delivered to my parents' home from America. 'I am sorry, but you'll have to do it if that's what you want. Phone them up for help for Dad.'

My response to this, as you can imagine, was complete and utter amazement. What I responded is too explicit to put in this book, but you can imagine what you would have said to your own so-called brother.

I was left speechless and bewildered. When I told my friends the response that I had received, they were also at a loss for words, which left me with a far more difficult choice to make. After an unsettling night of mental strains and confusion, I resumed my fourth day of inductions on a life-changing new job. It meant good money and good future prospects to create a better life for myself, earning a decent wage. I made a decision that tested my will and ability as a son: I stood up in front of a group of people, my friends included, and thanked them for giving me the job and also giving my friends the job opportunity I got for them. I thanked my friends for their support, and I thanked the management and other appropriate people, telling them that I had to return home and sort social services out, getting home help for my poor elderly father.

I packed up my belongings and returned home. I was full of utter anger and disgust at my brother and his lack of support for not so much me but for our elderly parents, who needed all the support that they could get from their offspring. Again, I am my parents' youngest child. I have two sisters, who are much older, and two brothers. The two sisters hadn't spoken to my mother and father in over twenty years. They walked past my parents' home on a daily basis and never once made an effort to patch up a falling-out over my wedding nearly twenty years earlier.

My sisters can rot in hell for the way they treated my parents. I have never regarded them as sisters, just as two very hateful adults with kids of their own, whose children have their own kids, which made my parents great grandparents. My mam and dad passed away having never seen their great grandchildren, which broke their hearts for twenty years. I have nothing but utter hate and disgust for these sisters. How could anyone live their lives and walk right past their parents' home daily with their children and grandchildren? They should hang their heads in shame and will always be shown utter contempt from me.

To give you an idea of my hate for them, if I ever passed them, I'd wish for them to die. That's an awful thing to say, but when you become a single person who has given everything for his parents and you have to listen for twenty years about the heartache they have suffered from their sons and daughters, it makes your blood boil. As your parents' youngest child, you and you alone have to pick up the pieces now. To do this for so many years breaks you down and fills you with hate. I know this is diverting away from PTSD, but it is all related, which will become apparent as this journey unfolds, so please be patient and read on.

I have two brothers. The oldest is called Donnie, and the other is Spencer. I have already spoken of Donnie, who is twenty years older than I. He abandoned my parents before I was born. He ran away from home at the age of 16 and came back years later to inform my parents that he was living in Holland. To be truthful, I know very little about him and his family. What I do know I will explain later on in my journey. And the other brother I have spoken about already.

Now that I had sacrificed my job and career to get things in place for my father, to start with up on my arrival home, I could see the instant change in my father's eyes, knowing I had returned to be home. This would lead to me becoming a full-time carer for him. He was now in safe hands and knew that their one true child (me) truly cared for them. He now knew that he would be able to go to the nursing home every day twice a day, and this was important for me, as I wanted to try to keep things as family-like as possible.

I arranged an appointment and saw a woman from social services, which was based in, funnily enough, the same place where my brother Spencer's children lived (who again, passes there for his kids twice a week). I discussed with her the needs I was seeking,what kind of help they could offer. I explained that I needed help with my father's care and was looking for help to keep him at home and not have him put in a nursing home. The woman from social services sat and listened to my plight as I explained that I had given my career up and come home to be a carer. This meeting took about an hour, and the day after, she and someone else came for a home visit at my father's home with me present. They did their assessment and helped me with a few other things. We got a lot put in place for making my father's life easier and more comfortable in these difficult times.

They were understanding and within days had a home helper come on a daily basis twice a day for breakfast and tea time and general visits to check up on him. They became vital in the help of my keeping him fit and healthy and well enough to stay at the family home. He quickly adapted to having someone there with him to help him around the house and so forth, also giving him comfort when I was not there.

To quickly recap, it took me less than an hour to organise social services for their help in implementing daily help, meals, hoovering, doing bits of shopping and general housekeeping. The comfort and company was most welcomed by my father. They helped organise a grant for central heating to be installed for him in the family home, as he was now having to sleep downstairs. I brought the bed down from upstairs and made it up so he was comfortable in one of the living rooms. I did try to get a stairlift installed for him, but because of the design of the house, this was impossible.

It did not take much of my time to get all this done after leaving my job and returning home to where I was born and brought up. It would have taken my brother less time to do than it took him to give me all of his excuses. What a complete waste of a person when there is a lack of love and respect for the parents that brought him into this world.

With things now in place for my father, I began to settle into the daily routine that was to become my way of life for the next five years. On a daily basis, I would go to my father's home and pick him up to go to see my mother at the nursing home where she now was living. This was where a fresh daily trauma truly began—to have to go to a place like this on a daily basis, taking an elderly father to see his only love in life. To have to undergo the trauma of this was completely soul-destroying; sitting in the lounge of the nursing home to visit a loved one was one of the daily traumas that ensued. Upon arriving in the nursing home, I would have to mentally challenge the mind and soul to absorb what I was about to go through. As a young man (age 35), I was not prepared for this.

I will now explain in detail the typical day of having to visit my elderly beautiful, loving, caring mother. It would begin with collecting my father from the family home. I would help him into my car, put his seat belt on, and start the short five-minute journey to the nursing home. My father— bless him—would immediately ask the question of when she would be coming home. By this, he meant my mam, his wife of fifty-seven years, his only love, his life, his soulmate, his beloved Freya.

I would have to find some sort of answer to give him. I would often say, 'We will ask and find out from the nursing home, Dad.' His getting his hopes up was utter and complete mental torture for me as a son to have to see. That look on my father's face, thinking that his wife may be allowed home at some point in the near future, was destroying my soul to its core. I had no proper answers for him, only words of comfort.

We would arrive at the nursing home and pull into the car park, and I'd assist my father out of the car, helping him walk to the entrance and taking myself a deep breath as I tried to search for the strength and courage to enter my daily visit to hell. We would sign in and be welcomed by staff, who would tell us if my mother was in the lounge or in her bedroom. Most days she would be in the lounge with the other residents who were in the nursing home. I would pull up a chair for my father, and he'd sit close to my mam. I'd pull myself up a chair and give my mother a loving kiss and a cuddle.

Things would be OK for a while, and then things would start to go wrong when my mother— bless her—would again start to say things such as that she had a busy day at work and just got off the bus. She would think she was at home with Dad and me and that things were normal; I suppose in her mind, things were.

My father would say, 'You have not been to work, Freya, and you didn't get off the bus. You are in a nursing home.'

My mother would look around her surroundings and see that she was not home; she was surrounded by strangers, other frail men and women who would often come up to me and mistake me for their own flesh and blood. They would want me to sit and talk with them, while all that was going on in my mind was wanting to pick my mother up, cradle her in my arms, put her in the car with Dad, and drive her back to our family home. I wanted to make things right and normal for them both to live together as they did before she had her fall.

I used to get strong mixed and confusing emotions whilst in the nursing home. My heart was broken knowing that my mother would never be returning to the family home to be with her husband. She would often go on about my brothers and sisters. She would say how she hated them for the way that they had abandoned her and Dad for the last sixteen-plus years of their lives. My blood used to boil at this point. I would start to think of how much hate I also had towards my siblings. There is no love lost between them and me. I had never grown up having a close relationship with my brothers and sisters, and what this did to my parents over the years, for them to only really have one out of five children who was there for them, broke their hearts and continued to do so for the remainder of their days.

Things in the nursing home would then go from this situation to me being confused, scared, and an emotional physical wreck to having to then go through further heartache when it would be time for my father and me and to leave the nursing home. My mind knew what was coming next, something that I dreaded daily. After having sat for three or four hours, I would have to start explaining to my father that it was time for us to leave. My heart would begin to fill with pain at what was to come next. My father would ask me to ask the staff how Freya was and if she could return home with him. At this stage, I would get up from my seat and walk out to see the staff, and they knew what was coming, like all the days before this day. I knew it was to no avail, and the heart breaking question that I found myself asking is, Will my mam ever return home?

I already knew the answer, so while my father was still sharing time with Mam, the staff knew how I was feeling and that my dad was expecting me to ask them the question. They used to open my mother's locked bedroom door and allow me to go in there and have time to myself. I would sit on my mother's bed and hold something that belonged to her. I'd cry my eyes out. My heart was broken, unfixable. I was an emotional wreck. Staff would often come in and comfort me and chat with me. Although this was comforting at the time, I knew I still had to pick myself up and go back to the lounge, where my mother and father would still be sitting there holding hands, still very much in love after all the years of marriage.

I would sit down and have further heartache to face. I'd have to look into my father's eyes and tell him why my mother couldn't come home today. This would then lead to another battle of pain and fears. My poor frail mother would then be aware that we would have to leave shortly, but as she suffered with dementia and was unable to walk at all, her mind used to tell her differently. She would always say, 'Right. Are we ready, son? Let's go.' These words were like being stabbed in the heart, leaving me feeling helpless and wishing that I had other siblings to help me with these burdens. But I knew was never going to happen.

I would comfort my mother and explain why she was in this place of unfamiliarity, this cold place filled with sorrow and foul smells of the elderly, poor people like my mother who could no longer live in their family homes and needed the care of a nursing home. In a way, some people were worse off than my mother was, but all were in there for the reason: full-time care. They had to be picked up, dressed, taken to the toilet, helped with food and drinks. Some would foul themselves, and most had to wear adult nappies.

I would explain to my mam that I was trying my best to get help so I could take her home to live once again with dad in the family home and to make things normal again. This would help comfort her. Then I'd give her a huge cuddle and a kiss. My dad would do the same, and then I would help my father out of the chair. We'd say our goodbyes to my mam and then make our way to the exit. In the background, all I would hear would be the heartbreaking words of my mother shouting, 'Ronnie, Daniel, take me home!' I would often get my father out of the reception area as quickly as possible to save him from hearing her screams for help.

We would then say a goodbye to members of staff after my father had spoken to them for a while. My dad would talk to anyone. He would often ask the staff himself when she would be able to come home. They used to be reassuring to him and say, 'Let's see in a few weeks or so. Let's see if we can get Freya up and about walking.' This, I could see, would comfort my father and would often ease some pressure off me. Dad and I would sign the visitors' book to sign out. As I did this, I always went through the visitors' book to see if my so-called brother had been there to visit, and I was never surprised that his name was never there.

I would hold Dad's arm and walk him to my car. Once we returned to the family home, I would get him settled in the house and stay with him for a few hours. I'd make tea, have a hoover around, and walk his little dog, which he loved to bits. I would see to other things before telling him I would return later in the same day and we would go back to the nursing home and see Mam again. But my day was far from over.

My father's sister, my auntie Meredith, lived just around the corner from my dad, and she was around the age of 90 at this time. I would walk round from my dad's house and go see to her. I would go get her pension shopping and pay her bills. I had now found myself becoming a full-time carer for all of my family that I loved: my dad, auntie, and mam.

After doing Auntie Meredith's shopping, I would walk back round to my dad's house to reassure him that I would return later to go back to the nursing home. I used to feel bad, but he was OK around the house and always had home help coming in to see him daily.

I would now return home to where I was living at the time to further complications and to further despair. I was living in a two-bedroom house with a lovely front and back garden. I had a drive and a garage for my car. This was the home where I lived when I was married and my daughter was brought into the world. I had lived there alone, as I was divorced years earlier, but I had my daughter stay with me every weekend. This was our home up until Gabrielle turned thirteen. I had a new neighbour move in next door to the left of me. Things were fine with her initially but then things got strange and complicated for me, as if things were not bad enough in my life already.

My new neighbour turned out to be a complete and utter headcase. I think back now and think she resented me having a house to myself to bring my daughter up in, not taking into account that I had live there for over thirteen years before she moved in. I was a well-respected person in my community. All the people in the area knew me, respected me as a person, and were kind to me. The headcase that the council moved in next to me became an utter monster to my daughter and me. I will explain the complications as I go on, but I have to also add that at this time in my life, with my mother in a nursing home and my dad struggling to cope at home, I had no siblings or other family for support or to fall back. My ex-wife, the mother of Gabrielle, had complicated her own life. She'd met the wrong sort of bloke, a rough one, a known drug dealer at the time. She had moved him into her family home with my daughter and another child, Gabrielle's stepsister Ki, who was the daughter of the man my ex-wife left me for, the man my wife was wanting to take my daughter away from me to live with in London. This never happened, so now my daughter and his daughter were living with their mother and a monster who was a drug-dealing junkie.

As things were going on and I was being a carer and seeing my daughter every weekend without fail, I started to encounter problems with the headcase neighbour from next door. She sent her mother to my front door with two pumped-up steroid idiots and threatened my daughter and me. The mother of my neighbour accused me of having wild parties till three or four in the morning. What she was referring to was a BBQ I had with my daughter and a few friends. All had left my home by 9.30. My daughter and I were in bed by 11 p.m. at the latest.

The mother then proceeded to accuse me and blame me for her daughter having to go to the doctor and the doctor subsequently putting her on antidepressant tablets. This was complete and utter rubbish. A close family friend in the neighbourhood where I lived was a wonderful woman and had seen what was going on at my door, and she came over to see me. I told her what had happened, and she was furious. She informed me that the headcase next door had been on tablets for depression for fifteen years.

Things from this point got worse with my neighbour, and on top of this, one weekend my daughter was staying with me on a Saturday night just before my birthday. We'd both retired to bed and were awakened at 11.45 p.m. by the police knocking at my door. I made my way down the stairs. With my disability at the time, I was virtually disabled on the left side of my body (from the trapped sciatic nerve).

Upon answering the door to the police, my daughter was awake and at the top of the stairs, looking down at me talking to the police. I was expecting further bad news, perhaps something to do with my mam or dad. As they began to explain why they were there, I could not believe what they told me. They asked if I was the father of Gabrielle. I said yes, that she was staying there with me now. They informed me that they had with them in the police vehicle my daughter's mother and asked if she could come in and stay there with her two dogs, as the junkie roughneck she was with had beaten the living daylights out of her.

I agreed to let them bring her into my home, as my 12-year-old daughter was there listening to her mother's name being mentioned. The officer went to his van. I asked Gabrielle to go down to the front room, where I sat her down and told her that her mother had been assaulted and that the police had brought her to my home for her safety. The police brought her mother into my home, and Gabrielle and I were not prepared for what we saw. The poor lass, my daughter's mother, my ex-wife, had been severely beaten by this complete and utter thug.

Instantly, I felt uncomfortable, as we had been divorced for over ten years. Now here she was in my home, where we as a couple had brought Gabrielle, our daughter, into the world. I got her settled and asked what on earth she had gotten herself into. She began to explain and then asked me to inform the man she'd left me for that she was here with me and that he was to keep Ki with him, as he had her staying overnight at his home.

I recall looking back and thinking, *This is all I need. I have severe nerve damage and can hardly walk, my mother is in a nursing home, and I'm struggling to keep my father fit and well. I have problems with a crazy neighbour, no siblings to support me, and now this with my ex-wife … How could things possibly get any worse? Why are bad things happening to me?*

Yet this was only the beginning of more bad things starting to happen in my life. I do hope you are still here with me on this journey as I unfold my life to you. If you are intrigued so far, then stick with me, please, as things have not yet even begun to start to unfold; things started to get ever more complicated for me. All I can say at this point is to continue reading, as all that you have read so far is the slow build-up to my being diagnosed with PTSD, how things have turned out, and how I have overcome so many difficult traumas.

I think that it is important for you to understand my state of mind and the problems I have had to bear. You will eventually read about the finishing hurdle and the last pages of my journey of life so far. You will find yourself having a further and greater understanding of your own life, your own difficulties, and the help that is available to you as a sufferer of depression, anxiety, or PTSD. I will show you that there is a light at the end of the dark tunnel of life lying ahead of you; it may well help give you an understanding of the underestimated illness that you suffer from as a person with PTSD.

So I now had my ex-wife in my home with Gabrielle and me, asking her what had gone on and so forth. At this point, I must state that I did not know who she was seeing, as I had nothing to do with her life. I used to pick my daughter up and take her to my home, where we would have a good weekend together, so upon finding out that she had split up with the man she'd left me for and was now with this other person, things became apparent that she was involved with the wrong kind of person. It was becoming more and more concerning. I spoke to Gabrielle's stepsister's dad and informed him that I got my daughter and her mam settled in my bedroom. I slept downstairs.

The next morning, my daughter and her mam wished to return to her own home, but because of concerns about my daughter's well-being, I insisted that Gabrielle stay with me until things were sorted out. I also spoke with my daughter's stepsister's father and informed him what was going on, saying that Gabrielle was to stay with me for the time being. He made the same decision and kept Ki with him at his flat.

The same day, the police came back to see me and discussed what had gone on, the nature of the assault, and the person who did it. They gave me background knowledge of what he was like. Soon it became apparent to me that Gabrielle was to stay with me until police and also social services were happy that my daughter's mam was no longer with this violent man and that he was no longer in her home and living with her, where my daughter or Ki would be.

As things went on, I was coping as best as I could with life and what was being thrust upon me: having to be a carer for my dad and my auntie and now having Gabrielle living with me, not to mention the ongoing problems with my neighbour and with my daughter's mam and her still having her abusive boyfriend staying at the family home and social services being involved with my life and my daughter's. I recall that Gabrielle's mam's first assault was near my birthday, so that was October. We were now approaching Christmas Eve, with Gabrielle still with me and Ki with her father.

I had the police knocking at my door with yet again more bad news about my daughter's mam. She was with them again in their car, and police wanted her to stay at mine because this social degenerate, this thug, a bully of women, had assaulted her yet again. I had no choice but to agree for her to come in, and the shock was written all over my face. He had beaten her to a pulp, and the police informed me that if it were not for the sake of her two dogs attacking her abusive boyfriend while he was jumping on her face that she could easily have been killed that night. So I now had the blood-soaked mother of my daughter back in my home on Christmas Eve. My daughter was inconsolable and distraught at what she had seen.

We managed to get through that night and went out the next night, Christmas Day, to witness heartache with having to see my mother in a nursing home for the first time and not at home. Gabrielle and I spent time there with my father and mother while trying to keep things family-like and as close to a normal Christmas Day as possible. While we were sharing time with my mother, my brother Spencer turned up to see my mother, so I left my dad with my mam and with Spencer and his girlfriend for him to take my father home so I could go spend some time with my daughter.

We saw my auntie Meredith and spent time wishing her well. We left Auntie Meredith's to return to our home of thirteen years to find that all my windows had been smashed. There was glass everywhere. Christmas was ruined. What a true trauma in itself. My ex was back at her house. I phoned the police to my home, my crazy neighbour from hell was at this stage having a good old shout at my daughter and me, saying things like, 'Yeah, you fucking deserve that. Have a good Christmas.' What a cold-hearted *bitch*.

Gabrielle and I went indoors to wait for the police to come. We cleaned up as best we could. The police arrived on Christmas Day and did their job, but there were no witnesses as to what happened. The council came and boarded all my broken windows. I sat up with my daughter and consoled her. We talked about her mother and why she couldn't go home to her mother's and stay with her and her sister. I explained to her that it was unsafe for her while her mother was lying to us, the police, and social services, saying she was not with her boyfriend anymore. But she was, as we had seen her travelling in a car with him when she should have been nowhere near him.

By this time on Christmas night, we were rather settled a bit after everything that had gone on, and we were put through the grinding mill again. We had another brick come through the window, the only remaining unbroken one left. The brick nearly smashed into my daughter's head. I ran with my knackered back and damaged leg, screaming for the cowards to come back and be real man and fight me, but no one was to be seen. The police called again, and the council came back with more boarding up. My child of thirteen was in total shock and completely scared. My lunatic neighbour was at it again. I was on the verge of losing the plot. I was stressed and exhausted. Gabrielle, by this stage, was too afraid to sleep in her own room, so she shared my bedroom. I brought her bed into my room, and we then fell asleep.

To protect my daughter and myself, I had a security light installed, along with a CCTV camera which had motion detection enabled so If anyone walked past the front of my house, the light would come on and the TV would switch over to a tuned in Channel and. I could then see who was walking past my home instantly. This settled Gabrielle's and my nerves a bit. A couple of days passed, and we had a meeting with the council. They came round and installed unbreakable windows made of high-resign plastic. Things settled down for a while.

The new year arrived, bringing with it more complications. My ex-wife's boyfriend, the low life that he was, came over one night while I was at my mother's nursing home visiting her. He cut through the wires of my CCTV camera and ripped it off the wall. I installed another one and then phoned some friends. At this stage, he was also targeting Ki's dad, breaking windows and causing heartache. I ended up having the man my wife had left me for living with me in my home with Ki so we could keep Gabrielle and her sister together.

We contacted some friends and went on the hunt for the low life of a man one night. Now, this man was a man who beat women to a pulp and left ropes with a noose in them, along with a carving knife and notes threatening to murder my daughter's mother. This was why, as a parent, I would not allow Gabrielle back home to her mother's.

My friends and I and went hunting for this scumbag to give him the biggest beating of his life. We went to my ex's house to look there. But he should not have there, as my ex was at this stage of her life trying to prove her love for her children and getting them home safely, as social services were keeping a watchful eye over her. Yet we went there on a daft hunch to look for this predator, this violent woman-beating scum, and behold, he was there. Things went mad, and he fled, making an exit from the house, and scurrying off like a coward. I screamed for the coward to come and fight me. Remember, I was disabled. I shouted, 'What are you afraid of you, fucking coward!' But it was to no avail.

Whatever we'd done that night worked, as he left the area and was not seen since. Things seemed to become a little better, and I settled into the routine of having Gabrielle living with me and having Ki and her dad staying a lot of the time. I started the daily routine of getting Gabrielle to school and then going to pick my father up to go to the nursing home in the morning and again in the evening, with Gabrielle with us, which made my mother and father happy, as they didn't see any of their other grandchildren, which there were a lot of. I found find this extremely difficult, as was a hard enough place for me as an adult to go to and see my mother, but to have to take Gabrielle there for her to witness what went on there and how poorly people were treated. She coped with it well for a child of thirteen, remarkably well. What a wonderful strong young girl she was. I was proud of her and the person she had become.

So things were settling a bit and life was passing by. The next thing I knew, I was at court regarding Gabrielle's mam and the well-being of the children. I had convinced myself that the best place for Gabrielle and Ki was with their fathers, but social services and the courts had other ideas. Their plan was for the children to return to their mother, and for their safety, they were forced to relocate out of the area they had grown up in for the last thirteen years to a place that the courts thought seemed to suit their needs and provided safety for my ex and the children so that my ex-wife's boyfriend could never find out where they were. The courts were expecting me to live miles away from my own flesh and blood and not know about their lives. Well, this was something that was not going to happen.

I refused to leave the hearing until I had an address of where my daughter was going to be forced to live and lose all contact with the friends she had grown up with and the schools where she was doing well. To unsettle them and their education was a bitter pill to swallow, but the judge had made his rulings, along with the social worker, who was a horrible woman who later betrayed my confidentiality.

My daughter was now living miles away, and it was difficult to see her, but I managed to get on with things. A year passed, and things became a strain again. I was now forced out of my home of fourteen years, thanks to my lunatic neighbour and her drug-dealing relations from the next village. A friend offered me his flat to stay at for a while as I tried to organise a new place to live for my daughter and me. As if life were not bad enough with my mam, dad, and auntie … But I had no choice. My daughter would no longer stay in the family home she was brought up in, and with the neighbour from hell causing me lots of problems, I went ahead and stayed in one of my good friends flat for a while to assess my options and to see if I would ever wish to return to my own home.

I went camping one night for a break with my close friend Stan. He was a good lad. We didn't go far, only up our local nature reserve. We got a fire going, had a few beers, and I got a phone call from a neighbour near my home. At this time, I had let a friend stay in my house, as he was homeless. He was a handy person and could handle himself well. So he was in my house, I was in a friend's flat, and the phone call was from Jay and Jo, a lovely couple who had witnessed my plight in my home. Jo proceeded to inform me that there were roughly about fifteen thugs at my door, all armed with baseball bats, knives, axes, and pieces of metal bars, and they were trying to smash my house to bits. My friend who was staying there at the time was thankfully unharmed, and they could not get in due to the unbreakable windows installed.

I immediately told Stan to take me home; I would have to go sort it out.

And his words hit home and made me think: 'Fuck, it's only bricks and mortar; there is nothing you can do. Let go of it.' And he was totally right. My daughter no longer wanted to stay there, thanks to my ex-partner's boyfriend and thanks to my neighbour from hell. When I returned there the day after camping, I went to see Jay and Jo, and as soon as I got there, they informed me that my neighbour and her boyfriend were there with the gang of thugs and that she and her bloke were also armed with a weapon to get into my home and do God knows what damage to myself and daughter if we were there—or to my friend who was staying there.

No sooner had I arrived at Jay and Jo's whom were close friends and looked out for me as soon as I arrived to there home to see what had happened the night before the crazy next door neighbour who was causing me problems phoned her relations. They arrived in minutes. I instantly thought that this was a good severe beating and that I was going to get at least eight people, including my neighbour and her boyfriend. I grabbed the nearest object and went outside of Jay and Jo's, home and approached the gang of lads that my crazy neighbour had brought to my home the night before and I was prepared and ready for a good beating. As I approached the gang, whom my crazy neighbour who lived directly next door to my house had brought up again I asked them if it was those at my house with weapons the night before they replied it was and that they wanted to know whom the lad was who was staying in my house. I told them no names and asked them if they had been the ones trying to smash my house to bits and cause damage. The answer was yes and that it would continue until I left the area.

I went down the right law-abiding procedure. I rang the police and put a report in. I informed council about my plight with my neighbour and what had happened. My other neighbours all reported this and supported my claims, yet the authorities decided to let me down, and as a result, the thugs won and I lost my lovely home of more than fourteen years.

I was now left struggling to find somewhere for my daughter and me to stay as well as looking after my father and mother and my auntie. How could things possibly get any worse? Well, worse they got—and in bigger proportions.

I now found myself doing an exchange for my two-bedroom house for a two-bedroom first-floor flat. The girl I exchanged with was my ex-girlfriend's sister and her husband and daughter. These people were wonderful but were also at the time having problems with their own neighbours. Her husband was Turkish, and they were living in a one-bedroom upstairs flat with a newborn. The downstairs people were young junkie drug heads, and they would constantly cause a disturbance for her and her husband. They even tried setting their flat on fire while they were inside. What a fucked-up society we live in.

Anyway, they were offered the flat I was living in now, and I gave them my old house. However, I made sure it was what they wanted, informing them about the lunatic neighbour and what she had done to me. They made their minds up and thought nothing about it. The exchange was done. I truly hoped that they had no chew from the lunatic next door and that she would not cause a young couple with a child the problems she caused me.

As time went on, that proved to be wrong. She had caused endless problems for her and her husband. What a twisted bitch this neighbour was. But I tried not to look at things too much; after all, I was out of there and in a new two-bedroom first-floor flat. What could possibly go wrong there? Well, yes, you guessed right. I had moved from bad to worse, and I now find myself stuck above a lad below me who was a junkie crack addict who liked to sit up all night playing music, shouting, and screaming at the top of his voice while off his head on drugs all night long.

I threatened him that I had involved the council now and they were involved for three years regarding this problem and nothing was getting done. The council honestly didn't care about the hard-working normal people in our society. They were more concerned about the low-life junkie crack addicts who didn't give a damn about society other than to rob it and to inflict pain and suffering on decent people. The council's feeling was that we were getting full rent for the property, as they didn't work, so all their housing benefits paid for their rent and council tax, just for them to stay in these homes and destroys people's lives.

My current neighbour was a nightmare. He had people smashing his flat to pieces. He'd go through windows on a regular basis. His front door and frame had to be replaced at the cost of thousands, just for the council to say, 'Get yourself back in there. We have slapped your hands. Go annoy the world with your junkie crackhead friends and girlfriend.' She was also a junkie. This country is a shameful disgrace to live in, and I will be glad when the day comes that I can leave it.

I began to settle into my new flat and started to relax away from the problems of my old home. My daughter was moved out of the area with her mother for their own safety, and now I found myself adjusting to the difficulties of my beautiful daughter living miles away and fitting into the daily routines of being a full-time career. I went twice a day every day to take my father to the nursing home to share time with my mother. I would leave the nursing home and go around to Auntie Meredith's to see to her needs, such as doing the shopping, paying the bills, and doing housework and other related chores she may have wanted done.

The hospital contacted to schedule the major surgery on my trapped nerve in my spine. I instantly began the questions of how long I would be in for and what abilities I would have once I had the surgery. The surgeon went through this with me in detail and explained that I would be in hospital for at least two to three days and that the recovery would take many months, a minimum of eight months, he told me. My reaction was that I could not let it take that long! My mind was asking the question as to how my father would cope. The same for my auntie. I had no one else to call on for support with getting their needs looked after. After the shopping, the bills, the taking my father to the nursing home … My head began to ache with the worry of it all. I was reluctant to agree to have the surgery. But the surgeon got me a booking.

While in the hospital, I thought, *I need to get out of here*. I began to realise that it was not long since I had spent every day and night for four months taking my father to see my mother. I then began to get mixed thoughts and feelings about being there.

I arranged for a quick exit from the hospital, on the way out having to pass the ward my mother was in. I had such a shocking feeling of sorrow and heartfelt pain about the hospital starting to take effect. I hurried out of the place passing ambulances, the deafening sounds of their sirens and blue flashing light s. I began to breathe faster and faster as I rushed as best I could with my damaged leg. I made a hurried rush to the car and left.

Making my way out of the car park and passing the A&E ward entrance, I began to have a flashback of the night my mother was brought to the A&E ward. The flashback was a vivid reminder of this traumatic night and the future problems I was still to face in time.

I was then at my father's house, explaining to him that I had to go in hospital for surgery soon to relieve the agonizing pain from my back. He panicked, and I told him not to worry; everything was going to be OK. My thoughts were coherent at this stage, in a sombre state, thinking about returning to hospital, where my mother was for four months or more.

I wondered who would take my dad to the nursing home every day, who would look after Auntie Meredith, and what I would do. Becoming ever more concerned about this, I told myself not to phone my brother; he had already proved that it was only about his own family. A friend of many years, who was also an ex-girlfriend, helped me through the times when I was in hospital. And after I had the surgery done, she was a truly wonderful woman whom I truly cared for.

The surgery now done, I didn't have time to hang about in getting better. I stepped up my recovery rate of walking and exercising, swimming, and so forth. I made excellent progress and was able to resume my full-time duties of looking after my family.

Now travelling thirty miles a weekend to have Gabrielle stay with me, things were going rather OK. A couple of years passed going to the nursing home to take my father and my daughter, also sharing anniversaries and Christmastimes at the nursing home, all the time wishing for my life to be different. During this time, I was in a relationship that was going well. Life was going on as usual.

It was in the year 2007 on my journey, which had been extremely difficult so far, as I think you would agree. Well, now the next Traumas I talk about in this book are going to completely blow your mind and heartstrings to pieces. In the coming chapters, I am going to explain my five traumas that changed my life forever.

CHAPTER 1

TRAUMA 1

The Passing of My Mother,
Freya Osborne, 80 Years of Age

It was now early 2007, and my father was not coping too well at home. I was doing all that I could to keep him in his home. I had social workers do home visits for further help with my dad. They helped as best they could. My life had suffered now for four years seeing the effects of dementia taking further grip of my mother. I had become an emotional wreck myself, but I was holding it together rather well under the circumstance. The toils of being the youngest son of five children and having to be a full-time carer were taking an effect on me. I started to feel real animosity towards all of my siblings for their lack of support and help for me as a carer and for my father and auntie.

This was the year my brother got married abroad. I got no invite to this wedding but was not expecting one. They had a second type of wedding reception after returning home, and my brother contacted me and asked if I would bring my father to the hotel for their reception, and I agreed. On that day, I went to pick my girlfriend up. We then went for my father and took him to my brother's reception. When we arrived, we were seated at a table on our own, just my father, my girlfriend, and me. We were the only members of our side of the family, and it was a strange affair, to be honest. I won't bore you with the details.

When it was time to go, we said goodbye and I took my father home, settled him in, and locked the doors for him. I then travelled with my girlfriend to where she lived, and we sat and discussed what we had just witnessed. In fact, she picked up on this first. But I thought the same way—why were we invited to that reception? And the conclusion we both agreed on was heart-breaking. My brother and his new wife wanted to use me to take my father to the reception for the simple fact to show that he had some sort of family. After all, there was only my dad and me from his side. I became enraged with hate. It was like having to parade an elderly father about to ease his guilt. He made my blood boil, and my girlfriend had to calm me down, as I was ready to explode.

Now, upon the days approaching this reception, I asked myself the question which if it was me in that circumstance and I was wanting my family there, I would not have had the wedding in the first place without having my mother there at my father's side on the night of the reception.

My mother may have been suffering with dementia, but my brother had told her he was getting married and that he was having a do. Even my poor father had to explain this to my mother, and they were both expecting to be there. How heartbroken my poor mother and father were.

As it was not my place to arrange their wedding function, they were left to get on with it. My father wished for his wife to be there, and I hoped the right thing would be done, but it never was.

The day after the wedding reception and the falseness of it, all the parading of showing my brother, his wife, and their friends and family that he had a father and a brother (me), I was bitterly angry. I wanted to punch his face to bits and show him what I really thought of him, as I now had to go and pick my father up and go to the nursing home and explain to my frail poor mother that my brother had had a wedding reception and that we were there last night. An already distraught wonderful mother's heart was broken and all the heartache on her face was soul-destroying. I know she wanted to go, and I hoped that my brother and wife would have done what any normal people would have done and arranged for the staff to have taken my mother there in an ambulance transport, staying with us while we were there. I knew they would do this, as I had asked the question beforehand in anticipation, thinking he would without question have his mother there. After all, my mother would never see another family wedding.

My mother and father could never forgive him for this, and I certainly never could. What a disgraceful act to have done to your own parent. No wonder they used to call him as bad as the other sons and daughters that abandoned them in their life.

The wedding now out of the way and the pieces put back together, the heartache and disappointment of it was forgotten as life returned to the daily routine of being a carer and going to the nursing home every day, twice a day, to look after my family. Further down the line, I split up from my girlfriend, as things were stretched too far with my being a carer, and having a normal relationship with her was extremely difficult to do under the circumstances.

Around June 2007, I got a phone call from the nursing home saying my mother had taken a turn for the worse and that they had called for an ambulance. I rushed down to pick my father up and explained what had happened while on the way to the nursing home. We arrived just ahead of the ambulance and made our way to the entrance. At this point, my mother was in her bedroom, and we made our way down there not knowing what to expect. My heart racing, I went into the room, where a member of the staff was comforting her. I sat and held her close to me as my father came in the room, assisted by staff.

The paramedics came in to assess her and informed us they would be taking her to our local hospital, which is where I had been not too long ago to have my surgery. I instantly felt my body becoming nervous and anxious about this intrusive image and reminders of my recent visits here with my mother and having surgery myself. I had to sit and compose myself to relax so that I could follow the ambulance with sirens and blue lights on.

We followed the ambulance, and the journey took us up to A&E, the exact journey my mother was taken on when she had her fall four years before, so I was on edge trying to comfort my father by telling him everything would be OK.

I swallowed my pride and phoned my brother to let him know what happened. We arrived at hospital and followed my mother to the A&E ward. I began to get cold shivers down my spine, an almost out-of-body feeling that all was not well. I began to recall and relive the intrusive images, sight, smells, and reminders of the night my mother was brought in four years ago and the four months spent here daily, bringing my father to visit my mother after her fall at home.

Doctors' and nurses' faces had become so familiar to me from previous times there. They took my mother into a cubicle. I could see the curtains drawn closed while they did their assessments of my mother. My dad and I sat waiting for my brother to turn up with his wife. They were acting all concerned. He sat and talked to my dad while I went for a walk to try to compose my feelings. We were called into the cubicle by doctors and told that they would be admitting my mother. It was the same ward, same faces, and the same smells. It was also the same room and bed that she was last in. My mind was taking a battering at this point. We got my mother settled in and sat with her for about four hours, until the staff asked us to leave.

I made the long, slow journey back out of ward 5 and to the elevators. My elderly father was bad on his legs, so we slowly made our way towards the main north entrance, where I helped my father sit down while I went to the car park and got my car to bring it to the north entrance so it wasn't far for me to get my father in to the car from there.

When we arrived back at my father's house, I helped get him settled and sorted out for bed. We sat and chatted, and I reassure him that everything was going to be OK and that Mam was in the best place while she was poorly.

Tucked in his bed with his little dog for warmth and comfort, I kissed him good night and returned to my flat. I was now alone in the loneliness of my flat, reflecting on what had just happened and having many intrusive images and reminders of A&E and ward 5. The smell of hospital was once again overpowering me. I headed straight for the shower, were I scrubbed myself of all the smells. Now showered, I sat in a chair and broke down in an uncontrollable flood of tears at the thought of my mother being ill in hospital. I cried myself to sleep. I was a broken and bewildered man, a lost soul.

The following morning came, and I had not had much sleep due to what was going on with the junkie neighbour downstairs, who was pushing his limits. I got myself ready and went down to my father's. He was up and awake, and the carer who helped from social services was there getting some breakfast ready for him. I walked the two minutes round the corner to my auntie Meredith's. She was now 94 years of age.

I began to explain to her that my mother had been taken to hospital the night before and was once again in ward 5. She asked how my mother was. I told her I was not sure yet but that the doctors would inform me when I went back to hospital. I told her to visit with Dad. Auntie Meredith insisted on wanting to visit my mother, so when visiting hour approached, I took my dad and auntie to the hospital. We made our way to ward 5 to see my mam. We sat and chatted with her for a while, and the doctor shortly turned up, informing us that my mother had pneumonia and was not well. We stayed for the three-hour visiting time and then made our way home.

I made the decision to ring my oldest brother, who lives in Holland, and inform him of our mother's condition. I don't know why I did this. It seemed right at the time, and my father wanted me to do this. He made the decision to travel overnight from Holland to come and visit our mother and father, whom he had not seen for at least eight years. I felt like a fool but agreed to pick him up once he arrived and bring him to stay at my father's. I took it upon myself to tell him what to expect and how frail our parents had become so he could be prepared to see them.

We arrived at my father's home, and my dad welcomed my brother, his eldest son, whom he not seen for many years. I then proceed to take my father and brother to hospital to visit my mother. We made our way to ward 5 to visit my mother. At this point, my brother left the room and went out into the corridor. I sat him down and asked what was on his mind. He said he was not prepared for what he had seen, how frail and elderly our mother and father had become. I recall that he broke down in tears. I sat and comforted him as best as I could. I told him to look into my eyes. I told him, 'This is what you and the rest of my brothers and sisters have abandoned and left to me, your youngest brother, to take care of. Welcome to the reality of what I have struggled on my own with all these years. You are all a disgrace to these loving elderly parents who brought you all into this world.'

I then told him to pick himself up, pull himself together, and go sit with our mother and father. I find it strange that as the youngest child of my parents, it was me who had to keep the family together and support them, without any support or love showed for me. No wonder I am filled with great hate and animosity towards my siblings.

After staying with Mother for the day, I took my father and brother home to my dad's house, where my brother would stay while here. What a waste of time, I was thinking, that I'd expected him to be some comfort for my father to share with one of his sons, yet what did my brother do for the duration of his stay? He spent it in the pub down the road from my father's home. What a waste of my time and effort. This proved he was no use to my father or me, and to be honest, I was glad when he was on his return journey back to Holland after his short stay of five days.

So I was now back to where I started, me alone taking care of my dad and auntie, taking them on daily visits to see my mother in hospital, along with doing their shopping, paying their bills, and so forth, as both my mother and father a few years prior to this time had arranged for me with solicitors to have power of attorney so I could get them their pensions and so forth. This was something that I never wanted put up on me, but the solicitors told me something that deep down I already knew. Who else was there to do this? My auntie never could have children, and my father had no one else. This is the reason that when they sorted things out with solicitors, they put my name down, as I had been caring for them anyway for the last four years.

With this done, we kept going on a daily basis, twice a day, to the hospital to see my mother. From the moment of getting into my car to arriving at the hospital, I would suffer many different emotions from being scared of the sights, sounds, and smells of the daily routine of my visits there.

The month of July 2007 passed, and my mother was still not getting better or improving enough to go back to the nursing home. I think deep down I was preparing myself for worse times to come. Forgive me now as I am writing this, as it's very emotional and hard for me to do without being in fits of tears, but here goes.

The day was now 3 August 2007. I got a phone call from the staff at the hospital that my mother's condition had taken a turn for the worse. I went and picked up my dad. I rang my brother and told him to meet me there and that Dad and I were already on our way. We arrived at the hospital once again. Walking through the corridors towards the lifts, my heart at this time was beating a thousand beats at a time. I was becoming very frightened of what lay before me. I told myself that I needed to pull myself together for Dad's sake. I needed to be strong for him.

We arrived on the first floor, and the elevator doors opened. I held him tightly, as he was bad on his legs. We entered ward 5, sterilised our hands with hand wash, and walked to my mother's side. I pulled up a chair for my father and got one for myself. We sat at her bedside and talked to her and comforted each other. Shortly after that my brother Spencer arrived. He sat with us.

The afternoon went slowly, as if time itself were stopping. My brain was now in overdrive. I began to look at my surroundings, which all seemed far too familiar. It was as if my brain were taking snapshots of images and faces of the surrounding people, a photographic reminder that was going to haunt and stay with me forever.

My father was an emotional wreck. My mother was still awake, but my brother and I thought it would be best if Dad were to go home and return later. I think we both knew at this point that things would get worse, and we were not sure how our father would cope in the coming situation. So my brother took him home, made him something to eat, and gave him a cup of tea. As for me, I never left my mother's side.

My brother returned around 6 p.m., maybe a little later. He was in and out of the room. My brother was on the phone to his wife, informing her of what was going on and how our mother was doing. As it approached 9 p.m., my brother left the room once more to make another phone call and left me alone with my mother. I recall looking out of the room my mother was in and seeing him walk off up the corridor holding his phone.

Things were silent at this point. There were no doctors, no nurses, and no staff walking about. I felt Mother's hands gripping mine ever so slightly. I turned and looked at her. She was giving me a loving smile. I looked deep into her eyes and told her how much I loved her and how much I would miss her. I promised that I would look after Dad and be there for him. I told her how much Gabrielle would miss her. I was still looking into her eyes and knew she heard my words, and she said to me, 'I love you, son.' She then sadly and peacefully passed away in my arms while I held her close to me.

I screamed for help repeatedly whilst holding my mother in my arms, and it felt like an eternity before someone heard my screams for help. A nurse came in first. I begged her to help me, and she buzzed the red button. My brother had heard my screams, and he came running to our mother's side. He knew that our mother had just passed away. I felt instant anger and hate towards him for leaving me to go through the passing of Mother on my own. I wanted to swing for him there and then.

I left my mother's bedside and walked out of the ward, a shattered and broken lost soul. My whole life had just been lost and torn apart. My mother, whom I had supported and loved all my life, had now left me to be in God's arms. I made my way outside and broke down in tears. One of the nurses from the ward had followed me to comfort me. I knew her, as I had gone to school with her. She gave me a shoulder to cry on.

I somehow made a phone call to my beloved daughter and informed her that her nana had just passed away. She broke down in tears, as did I again, and I recall her mother comforting her as the phone call ended. I was now wandering the hospital grounds, and then my brother Spencer came out to try to comfort me. I screamed at him, 'Why did you leave me alone for me to go through that on my own!'

He could not give me an answer; I suppose making the phone call could not be helped, as he didn't know what was to unfold. I actually felt sorry for him that he missed saying a final goodbye to our mother.

As I look back at that moment alone with my mother, I now think that this was how it was meant to be. This is how she would have wanted it, she and I alone together, saying a fond, loving farewell to one another. After all, I was the closest of all her sons and daughters.

My brother and I were now left with the decision of having to tell our beloved father that all he had loved for over sixty years of marriage had passed away. We both agreed that it would be best for him to do what he could, maybe find the comforting words to ease his heartache. I myself could not face doing it, as I had just lost my mother in my arms. I had just encountered my first true trauma. I was a devastated soul as I left the hospital and ward 5 and made my way to the nursing home where my mother was cared for. I broke the news to them, and they consoled me. I then asked if I could go into my mother's room to have a moment to myself. They opened my mother's door, and I recall picking things up that had belonged to my mam. I held them and broke down. I was now an emotional wreck and finding myself in my mam's bedroom, where she had spent the last years of her life away from her family home and loved ones.

After many hours sitting there in tears, I made my way home. My brother phoned me to tell me he was staying the night with my father and that he had broken the news to him. He put my dad on to the phone, and I told him how much I loved him and how sorry I was about our loss, saying that I would be down in the morning. I know I should have been there for him to console and comfort his broken heart, but I could not bear to look him in the eyes and tell him how he had just lost his wife, my mother, after promising him that everything was going to be OK. I just could not find the words and energy to do it at that point.

My brother spoke with me after I had talked to our dad, and he told me that he was there for Dad and that Dad was holding himself together. I assured him that I needed to be on my own after having Mother pass away in my arms. He understood, and I told him I would be down the following morning, saying to let me tell Auntie Meredith the bad news.

A restless night lay ahead of me. I was wandering around my flat dazed and confused; stress levels were now making my heart race. I found that my heart rate was increasing faster and faster. My already swollen eyes with the tears I had cried began to fill up once more. I collapsed onto my bed, grasping a photo of my mother, uncontrollable tears soaking my pillow.

I tried to close my eyes and sleep, but I couldn't settle. My eyes closed, but what hit me next, I was not prepared for. I now began to have intrusive flashing images, smells, the sounds of sirens and their flashing blue lights starting to invade my mind. I started to see images of my mother passing away in my arms, her smiling face looking up at me as she took her last breaths. I began to scream uncontrollably, my body soaked from head to toe in sweat. I felt I was struggling for air. Panic hit, and I passed out.

I fell asleep, but my sleep was disturbed. I woke up again screaming and covered in sweat. I'd had a nightmare. This was a truly terrifying experience. I had never in my life had a nightmare, and it was truly gut-wrenching. I had relived through this nightmare the day I had just suffered and the loss of my mother. I woke up at this point in the nightmare where my mother took her final breath. Scared and alone in my flat, I stayed awake, too frightened to close my eyes at the thought of another nightmare. Signs of daylight struck my face through the curtains and reality hit me. I now realised that this was the first day of the rest of my life without having my wonderful mother with me.

Looking out of my bedroom window at the world before me, pondering life and what it had taken away from me, I asked myself, *How can things get any worse for me? Why do bad things keep happening to me?* I mustered up some strength and showered the smells of hospital away from my body. Still confused and distraught, I dressed and took a few deep breaths, preparing myself to embrace and console my beloved and devastated father.

Making my way from my flat to my car for the five-minute journey to my father's home, I instead walked past my car and began to walk to his home. I was thinking that it might help me find the correct words to say to him, that I had let him down. I'd promised him that everything would be OK for him and that Mam would be fine, but I'd lost her and was heartbroken and lost for words.

Slowly making my way down to my dad's, I found myself with an overpowering urge to call upon my two sisters, who had never spoken with my parents for maybe twenty years, and tell them that I wished for them to have died and not my mother, the pair of horrible cows, vile and evil women who deserved nothing good to happen to them in this life. I took a seat on a bench and made the decision not to give them the satisfaction of seeing me as a broken man. After all, it's not what my mother and father would want to see me doing.

So I turned my attention to making my way to my father's. The ten-minute walk took me about forty-five minutes and I tried to find the words to comfort him. When I arrived at his home, I opened the door with my keys and walked into the front room. I went to my father and held him tight, beginning the process of telling him how heartbroken I was. I said how sorry I was that I'd broken my promise of telling him all would be fine with Mam. We shared a long and tender embrace, and my brother tried to hold us both and console us, but I pulled myself away and let him hold Dad. My stomach was churning, and I was feeling sick towards him for leaving me alone in the hospital to have to go through losing my mother. I took it upon myself to walk round the corner to go inform my auntie Meredith, now 94 years old, that we had lost my mother and that she had passed away peacefully in my arms.

I had keys for Auntie Meredith's bungalow. I rang the bell, calling, 'It's me, Daniel.' Auntie Meredith welcomed me and said to come in. I went into the front room, sat down beside her, and began to tell her about my mother. She broke down in tears. I comforted her, and we consoled each other. She asked how Ronnie (her brother, my father) was holding up. I told her that my brother was round there with him, that Dad was broken-hearted, but I told her he would be OK. He had me, just as he always had.

After comforting her, I made my way back to my dad's. My brother said he must go home and see to things there. I said OK and that Dad would be fine with me. He left Dad and me to console each other.

I asked Dad if he wanted me to inform anyone else. He replied, 'Yes, son. Will you let your brother in Holland know?' I agreed and found his phone number from my mother's little book of names and addresses that she had beside the phone. I made the phone call. Ellena, my brother's wife, answered, and I told her the unfortunate news about my mother. She informed me that my brother was abroad taking care of his new villa but was due home yesterday, 3 August 2007, the day my mother passed away. She was concerned that she had not heard from him, as his flight to Holland had landed on time and she could not contact him. There was no answer when she called his phone. I asked Ellena to ring me once she had spoken with him to inform him of his mother. She said she would, and I hung up the phone. I told my father what had transpired.

The day passed and then the night. I stayed with my father to keep him company. The following evening, I got a phone call from my brother's wife. She was upset, as she was still unable to ring my brother or find out where he was. She knew that he had returned from his villa, as she had rung the airport and he'd passed through arrivals OK. She was worried, as it was not like him not to call. She also told me that they are no longer married; they'd divorced few years earlier. I said, 'Well, we over here in England, his family, would not know this, as none of you over there ever bother to keep in touch with us.' Anyway, she said they still saw each other a lot, as he saw his kids a great deal too.

She said that she was thinking of informing the police and reporting him missing. I said, 'If that's what you feel you must do, then I would recommend that you do it.' I asked her to keep me informed, and she said she would. I didn't tell my father, as I didn't think he could cope with the news of it all at this stage.

My mind was now wondering what had happened to my estranged brother, the son who'd abandoned his parents at the age of 16 and was now in his late fifties. I began to think strange things. I wondered what had happened to him since getting off the plane in Holland and then going missing. It was like a sixth sense, as if it were meant to happen, as my mother never had a good word to say about him. Was this some sort of justice for how he had abandoned our parents?

Something felt quite strange and surreal about it happening the day my mother passed away. I felt that if something had happened, then it was what he deserved. Perhaps it was a divine intervention, some rather strange force at work, but I didn't believe in that sort of thing. There would be a good explanation, and he would show up fine and well. He might have been at a friend's or with a woman, as he was always a ladies' man.

The later conversation with his ex-wife was to prove my above thoughts about something strange happening to him on the same day as losing my mother. To this day, it remains unsolved.

My brother's ex-wife finally rang me and informed me that she had reported him missing. The police were looking for him. Three or four days later, she rang again and told me that the police had found him wandering the streets of Holland with no belongings on him, no passport, driving license, no phone, car abandoned, no laptop. Other belongings were missing. My brother had no recollection of where he was, where he had been, and who he was. He was taken to hospital.

His ex-wife kept me informed over the course of the week about what happened. It was odd and confusing. The doctors at the hospital examined him, giving him brain scans and so forth, but could give no real explanation as to what he was up to or what had happened to him. She informed me that he was now like a 58-year-old child, that he couldn't work again and that he would not be able to retire to his villa, as he would need to be cared for now. This was not the kind of care I was thinking, as I found out in time to come. To look at him, he was still himself, but he had childlike tendencies, which I will come back to later.

The focus was now directed towards funeral arrangements and registering my mother's death. These were organised and taken care of by my brother Spencer. He arranged to register my mother's death and sort that out. I went down the street from my father's house to the funeral parlour, a rather sombre place. I met with them, and the funeral details were organised. The date of burial was to be on 9 August 2007. The service was to be held at a church that was less than fifty meters away from my father's front door. After the service, my mother was to be buried at the local cemetery, which was less than a mile away.

Now things were in place and the funeral taken care of. I stayed with my father at his home to comfort him and look after him. A couple of days went by, and I decided to go to the funeral parlour and say a final goodbye to my mother. I did this alone, which felt right, as it was that way when she passed away. I took some photos of Gabrielle, Dad, and me. I also took some teddy bears that I had gotten her while she was in the nursing home. I placed these with her so she had Dad, Gabrielle, and me with her always. It ripped my heart to bits doing this and seeing her in a coffin. It was a truly traumatic experience, one never to be forgotten.

When the day of the funeral arrived, my daughter stayed with me and comforted me. She was a tower of strength for me. What a remarkable and beautiful daughter she had become.

The service in the church was a tender and loving affair. A large amount of people showed up and paid their respects, offering their deepest sympathy. The service lasted about an hour or so, and we then left the church. I don't recall any faces or words of sympathy from anyone. I struggled to keep things together but knew I must for the sake of my father and daughter.

We then got into the hearse and followed to where my mother would be laid to rest. We arrived at the cemetery, the priest said his words, and my mother was then laid to rest. (God bless, Mam. RIP.)

Afterward, I took some time for myself. I stood over my mother's coffin with my daughter holding me tight, our tears flowing like wild rivers. I prayed to God and asked him to care for my mother, asking him for no more bad things to happen to me; my soul had taken a battering over the years caring for my elderly mam, dad, and auntie Meredith. I could not cope with any more traumas. I hoped he heard my prayers.

We made our way to the car and went to a function room at the pub, where we had a wake in the honour of our beloved mother, wife, and grandmother, Freya Osborne. This was a hard thing to do, listening to people saying how sorry they were for our loss, but that's what funerals are about.

Out of his five children, my poor father had only my brother and me to comfort and console him. I truly started hating my sisters and other brother at this point. How could the callous, horrible, vile creatures abandon their elderly parents and not give a shit about them or speak to them in over twenty years? My heart and blood were boiling. I wanted this day to be over and wished not to have to go through a traumatic event again for years to come. I never wanted to see another ambulance or flashing blue lights, hear another siren, or be anywhere near hospitals again. My heart could not take much more suffering.

You may find yourself now having some sort of understanding of my life and the traumas I had suffered over the last years, with no help or support from my other siblings, and how much it affected me and broke me as a person. I asked God for no more traumas or bad luck to happen to me.

But God was not listening to my cries for help. I now close the story of my first life-changing trauma, the loss of my mother, Freya Osborne, who passed away peacefully in my arms on 3 August 2007.

CHAPTER 2

TRAUMA 2

The Loss of My Father, Ronnie Derick Osborne, 85 Years of Age

After the funeral of my mother, I started to focus my attention on looking after my father and auntie. I was staying with my father most days now and only went to my flat for necessities, to put lights on, and so forth.

It was a week after the funeral, and I sat with my father and discussed the issue of getting a headstone put in place for my mother. He agreed and told me to do whatever I thought would be right. There were no concerns over cost or things like that. We both loved my mother so much, and she was thought of so much in life that it was befitting to get a headstone that reflected these feeling for the wonderful, remarkable wife, mother, and grandmother she was.

I found a beautiful headstone in a heart shape, cradling and held by an angel. I showed my father, and he said just to make sure it was what I thought was right for my mam. I got the inscription done, and the headstone was commissioned and would be ready to be installed by 10 September 2007. So that was taken care of and just waiting to be placed above my mam, an angel to watch over her.

As time passed, I was doing all I could to comfort my father and also to look after my auntie Meredith, now 95 years old. Both of them showed remarkable strength and courage under the circumstances and were coping OK, or as well as can be expected, over the loss of our beloved Freya.

I heard from my brother's ex-wife once or twice, and she informed me that there were no changes in my eldest brother in Holland. My other brother, as usual, continued to get on with his own life and left all the caring of my dad and auntie to me to cope with on my own, as it has always been for all my life. I continued to see my daughter as often as possible, almost every weekend without fail.

On 10 September 2007, I got a phone call to meet the stonemasons down at the cemetery, which I had been going to every day to be close to my mother and talk to her. I'd tell her how Dad, Auntie Meredith, and Gabrielle were are coping . I met with them, and they installed my mother's headstone. It turned out beautifully. My good friend at the time was with me, as she had also lost her mother in the same year. She was buried not far from my mother.

With the headstone now installed, they left, and my friend comforted me. She found it hard herself with the recent loss of her own mother, whom I knew very well. As we looked at my mother's headstone together, we stood back and noticed that the stonemasons had put the gold lettering of my mother's inscription on it at an obscure angle and it looked awful and made the headstone look like it was uneven and inaccurate which therefore made a beautiful headstone look terrible which filled me with anger as they had to remove it and take it away and replace it at a later date with another headstone which was the same headstone but with the lettering upon it with my mother's inscription made straight and not on a horrendous sloped angle so the heartache of my mother not having her headstone placed upon her at the first attempt was a difficult disappointing day but it was eventually replaced with their mistakes rectified and then the headstone really did look beautiful.

I got straight on the phone to them, angry as hell, and told them that they had a problem—and that problem was a grieving, angry son on the warpath over their incompetence. They immediately came straight back, and I showed them their mistake and the incompetence with such a delicate and heart-rending issue. They apologised and took my mother's headstone away to be replaced with a new one. I accepted this. It was replaced on 18 September 2007, the day before my father's eighty-fifth birthday.

The day of my father's birthday arrived, and I took him down to the cemetery and walked him to the headstone to show what I had done. I hoped he was proud of it and how I was trying to show how much she meant to him and me. He told me loved it and that it was befitting of Mam. We paid our respects and left, knowing that we had somewhere to go and pay our respects whenever we needed to, instead of just an empty bit of freshly dug soil.

My dad wanted my brother and me to go to the local social club for a drink with him for his birthday. He was a lifetime member there and was well respected. I agreed to go, although I felt nervous about going. Firstly, I was angry with my brother. Secondly, one of my sister's husbands worked there on the committee, and I could not be doing with his trying to comfort or offer his false sympathies towards my father or me. Why should I allow him to when they hadn't spoken with my mother, father, or me in such a long time?

In my eyes, his wife—my sister—had never given a toss about my parents for all these years, so why on earth should I listen to his pathetic, worthless sorrow towards us. He would be escorted away from my father if he came over to us, and I would tell him what I truly thought of him and my sisters.

My brother turned up at my dad's, and we made our way to the club in his car. We made our way in and sat down. A few people came over and offered their sympathy. The in-law was there, and I quietly made my way towards him on my way to the bar; my brother and father didn't see me. I warned him not to come anywhere near my father or me or he would regret it I also took it upon myself to tell him to tell his wife and my other sister that they'd better not ever cross my path.

I then returned to my seat with a round of drinks, and we tried to make a good night of it for the sake of my father. I took a few photos on my mobile of me sitting with him for his birthday. We had a fair night and made our way home.

My brother made his way back to his wife and home, and I got Dad settled. He was a bit tipsy. He got into bed, and the little dog jumped up on his bed with him. He fell asleep, and I made my way down to the cemetery. The time was now about 11.30 p.m. I sat for an hour or so at my mother's graveside and talked to her, telling her it was Dad's birthday and that he had a little drink with my brother and me. I told her how much Dad missed her and how heartbroken we all were at her leaving us to go to heaven.

In tears and distraught, I walked home to my flat and tried to go to sleep. I woke up screaming and soaked in sweat, the sheets soaked right through. I made myself a drink and ended up falling asleep on the sofa.

I woke up in the morning and got ready to go to my Dad's. I found him awake and chatting to the female carer who came in mornings to give him breakfast and make a brew for him. I left him chatting and went to Auntie Meredith's to see to her so I could do her shopping and so forth.

The next two days passed and it was now 22 September 2007. I was out getting a haircut, and I got a phone call from the woman carer who goes to my dad's. I could tell in her voice that something was not right. I asked what was up, and she told me that she had gone to see to my dad and that he was on the floor in the front room. She could not lift him off the floor or get him back onto his feet. I drove straight there and ran into the front room.

I helped her get him to his feet and seat him on the settee. I sat alongside him and asked him what had happened as I had my arms around him to comfort him. He told me that he had tripped but not to worry about the daft old bugger. He told me was OK. Then he collapsed in my arms, went limp, and was unable to talk well. But he told me he could see me OK but could not move.

I screamed at the carer to phone an ambulance. She rang for one, and when they arrived, the carer let them in. They asked what had happened. I told them. I also told them I was holding him in my arms and that I asked my dad what happened. I told them he spoke to me and then collapsed in my arms and could not speak. They took over, and I stood up to go into the kitchen, where I instantly screamed to myself in my head, *No, not fucking again! You can't take my dad away from me so shortly after losing my mam!* It had only been fifty days since she passed away.

My head was completely fried to bits, and mental exhaustion took a grip, but I managed to hold it together. I made the phone call to my brother and told him what had happened and that I was following them to the hospital. He said he would meet me there. The paramedics put my father into the ambulance, and once again, I followed them on the exact same journey that I had previously taken when my mother was taken to hospital. It was all too much for me to take in. I began to have intrusive flashbacks, images, and reminders of doing this before, the ruminating images hurting my head so much that I had to pull into a bus stop to compose myself. I took time to catch my breath and focus before resuming my journey, following the ambulance. When we arrived at hospital, I parked my car and ran to the entrance of A&E.

I walked into A&E and instantly became overwhelmed with emotions, a bitter sense of being here before in similar circumstance. My mind then began again with the flashbacks and the images of the day my mother was brought. The sounds and smells became all too familiar to me. My stomach churned, my heart sped up, and I was now traumatised with it all. I collapsed to my knees, and the images just kept coming and coming from my long months staying at my mother's bedside. My head ached so much, and I wished and prayed that everything would be OK with my dad. A nurse helped me to my feet and sat me down so I could compose myself while my father was being looked at.

The next thing I knew, my brother Spencer and his wife turned up. I told them Dad was in a cubicle being observed and that I needed to go outside for some fresh air. The nurse who'd helped me to my feet came out with me. She remembered me from weeks earlier, when I was there with my mother. She comforted me and told me she was sorry to hear about the loss of my mother. My brother showed his head and said we were allowed to go back through to our father's cubicle to be at his bedside and that the doctor would be with us shortly.

We went in and sat by our father's side, and shortly after that the doctor came in and told us that upon examining our father, he believed that Dad had suffered a massive stroke. I left the cubicle upon hearing this devastating news and sat in the reception of A&E. It slowly sunk in that my father had had the stroke in my arms in the home I grew up in.

I now rushed to a toilet and threw up. I once again became an utter wreck of a person. My life had just collapsed once again around me with my dad. I picked myself up from the toilet floor, washed the smell of sick away, and went back into my father's cubicle. The doctor proceeded to tell me that they would be transferring my father to ward 5.

The words hit me like a freight train. I started to have flashbacks of this ward, and they disturbed me so much that I fell to my knees again and sobbed my heart out, with no real comfort or words of support for me from my brother, as he was being consoled by his wife. I was thinking, *Not again. Not the same ward. What have I done to deserve this so shortly after my mother? How much more trauma must I have to suffer? How many more bad things are going to happen to me? I am a broken person with no real support for me other than from my daughter.*

My father was now moved to ward 5. I followed behind the hospital porter transferring my dad. I started looking at my surroundings. Each corridor that I passed through began to feel like a never-ending journey that was all too familiar to me. I glanced at certain pictures upon the walls of each corridor, and my eyes began to recognise each individual picture. It felt as if I had become like these pictures, affixed to these corridors. An overwhelming sense of knowing these walls and surroundings all too well overcame me. I feel as if I were a fixture of it myself. As I passed each picture, I began to feel overwhelmed and extremely anxious as I got closer and closer to ward 5, the ward where I had spent far too much time with my mother. I started to become tense, weak in the legs, with cold shivers running down my spine. My breathing became erratic, my vision became blurred, and I was fidgety.

I turned around the corner, aware of what awaited me, and then it hit me. My blurred tear-filled aching eyes glanced upon the sign I was dreading to see. Ward 5 flashed before me, and I was a total wreck at the sight of seeing the sign, but I mustered up the courage and walked into the ward. Doctors and nurses had now taken over from the porter. I was now thinking that I was back to where my life first fell apart with my mam, and I was hoping and praying that the doctors and nurses would not place my father back in the same room where I'd spent seven weeks or more comforting my mother with my dad. Anywhere other than this room …

My fears came true. My father was now in the same room where I'd watched my mother lose her life. I now realised that this could be where I lost my father. How much of a bad thing was I once again going to have to cope with and suffer on my own? When would bad things stop happening to me? What had I done to deserve all of this?

My father was settled into the room where we'd spent so much of our lives with my mam. I was instantly confused and unsettled with everything, like the corridors and all I was seeing. I became overwhelmed with emotion as I went into the corridor. I experienced something rather strange as

I glanced around and looked into the faces of hospital staff; each face that I looked upon became embedded in my head, almost as if I were looking at a movie in freeze-frame. Each face I glanced at was a face I knew too well. I could put a name to each of the faces that I passed. I was now having flashbacks, disturbing and upsetting images, thoughts, and reminders from my last encounter and the time there with my mother. I felt as I were going mad. Was I losing my mind? Was this normal? What was wrong with me?

Dad was made comfortable in his room. My brother, his wife, and I sat with him for as long as we are allowed. We held his hands, talked to him, and told him we loved him. We were soon kindly asked to leave and to come back during visiting times. So we made the long journey to the exit of the hospital. I told my brother that I would be returning to stay with Dad and that I would go round to Auntie Meredith's to let her know about her beloved brother and what had happened to him. Then we went our separate ways.

As I walked towards my car, I made the phone call to Gabrielle. I didn't know how to find the words to inform her of her granddad. I took my phone from my pocket and made the phone call, telling her what had happened. She broke down in floods of tears, as she was the closet of all grandchildren to my parents. She couldn't believe it was so soon after Nana. I told her that I knew and that I was a broken man lost for words. We offered each other loving words of comfort, and I told her I loved her so much, saying that when she wanted to come down and stay with me and go to the hospital to visit her granddad, I would pick her up. She said she would come down the next day.

I pulled out of the car park to make my way out of the hospital grounds, but doing this created further challenges for me. I now had to drive past A&E, where I had spent so much time of late. I took some deep gasps of air and started driving towards A&E, which I couldn't avoid because it had to be passed to exit the hospital. As I got closer and closer to it, I became overwhelmed once again. Feet away from the A&E doors, I was overpowered by approaching ambulances. Their blue lights hurt my eyes. The noise from the sirens hurt my ears, and the shape and distinction of the ambulances forced me to put my foot down to get away from there as quickly as possible.

The images and flashbacks that I experienced regarding the ambulances and their association were truly terrifying. Not only was this the second time of encountering ambulances, sirens, blue flashing lights, the A&E, and ward 5 but also with what I had encountered with my mother and father being taken to the same hospital.

I feel it is now appropriate to share another encounter that I suffered involving an ambulance in a road traffic accident which happened to me a few years earlier. I will try to keep this as brief as I can.

The year was 2005. Mother was in a care home, and the day was 2 January 2005. After spending my third Christmas with my Dad visiting his wife, my mother, I went down to pick my Dad up from his home to take him down to the nursing home to have some tea with my mother. The time was about 4.40 p.m. We set off down the road from my father's. I pulled up at a set of traffic lights that were on red at the time, and I was the first in line to drive through when they changed to green. It was dark because of the time of year. My dad was excited to go for some tea and see his wife.

When the lights changed to green, I set off as I had done millions of times beforehand. As you pull away from these lights, the only line of sight you have, as they are about ten yards back from the junction, is straight ahead of you. It's not possible to see anything coming from the left passenger side (your left line of sight) of you as you proceed through lights. I made my way through, and as I did, I heard nothing and saw no reflections of flashing blue lights approaching. All appeared normal. I got within a few yards of clearing, past the obstructed corner to my left, and as I went past the corner to proceed straight ahead, I was hit on the passenger side of my car by an ambulance speeding through a set of lights that were on red. This ambulance had no lights on or sirens sounding. I was broadsided by the ambulance, and the impact spun me a full 360 degrees. My car came to a halt from the impact.

I instantly turned to my father to see if he was OK, as the ambulance had struck the passenger side full on. Thankfully, he replied that he was OK, although obviously in shock, as was I. Leaping from my car, I took a look at the damage to where the ambulance struck. 'Thank God,' I recall saying, as I had managed somehow to pull away in the brief second of seeing the ambulance. It had struck the rear end of my car just behind my father's passenger seat. If a foot the other way, I dreaded to think what would have happened.

I now started screaming in rage towards the driver of the ambulance, a female driver with a male co-driver. After screaming at them, the ambulance pulled into a bus stop, as did I, to free the junction up, as it was congested with stuck traffic. The paramedics showed their profession and aid in my father while I paced up and down venting my anger towards them. I asked, 'What gives you the right to have jumped a set of red lights with no sirens or your flashing blue lights on to warn other road users of your presence?' They had no response and a year later were found guilty of reckless driving and endangering others.

Thankfully, there were no severe injuries to my father and me, but I was taken to hospital A&E for whiplash injuries. I was treated and discharged, and I made my way back to my father's. I was amazed that he came through it virtually unscathed. I made my way to the nursing home by taxi and informed the staff of what had just happened and for them not to tell my mother, as it would stress her and upset her.

The reasons that I am sharing all these experiences about ambulances, sirens, flashing blue lights, my traumas in my life, and so on, is that it's all information I am going to discuss in great detail regarding how I became diagnosed with (posttraumatic stress disorder and how I battled with it on my own now for 20 years. As you read further in the book about the PTSD I experienced, it will give you an understanding of the difficulties that I faced and perhaps the difficulties of your own trauma. I can truly say that if you finish this book, it will, without a shadow of a doubt, make sense to you. It may help you overcome your own difficulties as a sufferer of such a life-changing illness. Struggling with PTSD is an affliction that, in my eyes, goes unnoticed and with very little professional help or care other than private therapists.

To my knowledge, I know of no services within the UK NHS that can offer ongoing treatments. In writing my experiences down and sharing them fully with you, it would have been worth every hour of writing this book to help even just one person.

If it helps someone cope with the trauma of losing a loved one or being involved in an accident, if it helps give the reader a better understanding of PTSD and that you *can* and *will* overcome your difficulties that lay before you, you will know that there is a light at the end of the tunnel.

I will further talk about how I began to recognise my symptoms and how I sought the help to get me to where I am today. I look at myself daily and ask myself the question in the mirror as to how on earth I had survived what traumas I'd had, along with the bad luck I suffered. It truly has been a remarkable journey of life.

All that I offer in this book are raw detailed encounters of each trauma that befell me without the love and support of my family, the abandonment of my sisters and brothers, and the effects it took on my life. I will say right now that it's pushed me to the verge of complete and utter despair and self-destruction, an isolated person surrounded by no loved ones or support from my friends of late and of many years. The friendships would soon be put to the test, as explained on the pages to follow.

Hopefully, that has given you insight into my experiences so far with ambulances, hospitals, sirens, flashing blue lights, A&E, ward 5, and the traumas I have had to endure.

Back to my father, now in hospital ward 5, I picked up my daughter and she came down to see me to comfort me once again. It was such a burden for a young child of sixteen to have to bear. She gave me a loving cuddle, and we both shed tears. I took her to see Auntie Meredith, as I had arranged to take her with us to the hospital, yet again to see a loved one. We pulled up at the hospital, and I instantly became uncomfortable with the flashing images of late that compounded my brain once again.

Gabrielle took a tight hold of my hand, and I now focused my attention on how she must be feeling. How would she cope with seeing her beloved granddad in the same ward 5 as she did with her nana only weeks before? She and I got a wheelchair for Auntie Meredith, and then we made our way through the familiar corridors that we all had known far too well. We both comforted Auntie Meredith. Entering the elevator to go to the first floor, I prepared myself for what lay in front of me, as I now had my elderly aunt and young daughter with me and did not know how they would react, which frightened me. I put my senses on red alert for their reactions.

We entered the ward 5 entrance doors and used the hand sanitiser that is there to use. It always reminded me of hospitals from Mother's time there. The pungent smell of it would stick in my airways and wouldn't dissipate until I exited the hospital. It was a constant reminder of ward 5 and hospital, and I tried to block it out as we entered Dad's room.

Dad looked towards us as we entered the room. I gave him a loving embrace, as did Gabrielle, along with Auntie Meredith. He was unable to speak properly and could not use his left arm. We sat with him, telling him different things. I told him that I had taken his little pet dog to my flat so I could look after it for him until he was well enough to return home.

Saying this, I deep down wished that he would soon return home for me to look after him. He gripped my hand with his right arm and was clearly pleased that I was looking after his dog. I told him not to worry, that she would be fine with me and that I would be keeping a watchful eye over the family home daily. He tried to speak, but I was frustrated that I couldn't make out his worlds, so I spoke to the doctor looking after my dad. He explained the severity of my father's stroke. He informed me that he had suffered a huge stroke and would be unable to speak properly. He also said that the nurses had to use a suction type pipe to suction his throat, as he was unable to swallow properly. My heartache increased. (How much more would I have to cope with?)

I made my way back to my father's room, and we stayed the duration of allowed visiting times, until asked to leave. We kissed him good night and made our way out of ward 5 to the elevator and out of the main reception. Gabrielle stayed inside reception with Auntie Meredith, who was still seated in a wheelchair, so that I could go get my car to bring it to reception.

I walked to the car in a sombre state, upset and on edge. I brought the car to reception, and Gabrielle wheeled my auntie Meredith to the car. I helped her in and began to set off, knowing that it would again become a daily routine that I had to cope with. I drove towards the exit, passing A&E, and my senses were back on red alert. I now had to drive past the sight of ambulances, sirens, flashing blue lights, and so forth. To me, this was a truly traumatising experience each and every day for the next eight weeks, twice a day every day, without fail.

My life seemed to know nothing other than being traumatised by all that had befallen me. I now only felt despair, heartache, doom and gloom; I was on daily constant red alert and always on edge, unsettled in life, anxious, cautious, and distant from friends, constantly expecting and waiting for the next bad thing to happen to me.

As the weeks went by going to hospital and going through all the daily traumas I faced going there, I was put on an antidepressant from my doctor to help me cope with all that I was going through—the nightmares I had, the flashbacks, and the intrusive images, sounds, and smells. They were all reminders of bad things, and I was just barely managing to hold myself together. I had to try to keep strong. I had to care for my auntie Meredith and make sure she was OK and to ensure that nothing bad was going to happen with her.

It was now the end of November 2007, and my father's consultant asked to speak with my brother and me about my father. We went to see him at Hospital, where he told us that our father was showing no real signs of improvement. He wished to transfer him to a more specialised place for stroke victims. He told us he would be better cared for there, also saying that the place was only a few miles farther away from where my father's hospital was now. I agreed to this, as I had of heard of the place and knew where it was.

In a way, I felt somewhat relieved that I wouldn't be subjected to the daily traumas of the current hospital and its associations that I had become accustomed to for a total of five or months now. I was no longer going to be subjected to ambulances, sirens, their flashing blue lights, and their general shapes and sizes. I took some comfort from this. So my father was transferred to the new hospital. The two daily visits per day started there.

It was a better place to visit, as it did not have the pressures and associations or vivid reminders of the last hospital, so my anxiety levels eased a little, but it was still soul-destroying to see my father doing so poorly and unable to talk properly. I struggled to make out what he was saying when visiting, which was really frustrating for me. I used to get so upset at seeing nurses having to suction his throat and airways so that he could try to speak. I would try my best not to get frustrated with this, but when you have so much love for a father and mother as I do, your heart just wishes that you can take all their pain and suffering away and take it upon your own younger body to bear.

The coming weeks passed with no change, and I began to wonder how I was going to cope with my first ever Christmas without my mother here to share it with. My head was done in over the thought of it. I tried my best to be as normal as I could for Gabrielle's sake and for Auntie Meredith, but deep down the prospects of it approaching were ripping me apart. I had lost my mother four months ago, and having my poor father in hospital at Christmas meant nothing to me other than causing me to pray to God to let me make it over the festive time, a time for families to be united and close. I prayed for the strength to cope with it without my mam and my dad being poorly. All I asked for was to get it over with and to give my father the strength to see in the new year with me.

While I am writing now, my eyes are filled with tears, but I will struggle on, so bear with me, please.

I managed to spend Christmas Day seeing my father, Gabrielle, and Auntie Meredith, whom I took to see her brother. We all tried to keep things as normal as we could. I helped my father open the present that I got him—new pyjamas and slippers and a few other items which he looked upon with a soft smile. Gabrielle gave him the presents she had gotten for him. My brother was there with his wife, and we all shared a lovely day with my father.

The time came to leave, and we all kissed and cuddled him, telling him how much we loved him and that we would all see him soon. In fact, Gabrielle and I returned for the night-time visit on Christmas night, and we had a good time. We comforted him for as long as the visiting time allowed. Now that I was home, I thought, *Thank you, God, for letting me have this day with my dad.*

Gabrielle and I went down to the cemetery to pay our respects for my mother. We took a wreath which I had bought, along with a card, telling her how much we loved her and missed her and how heartbroken everyone is that she is no longer with us. I told her that I was lost without her and that Christmas would never be the same without her here to share it with. I told her that I had been to see Dad and spent the day there with him with Gabrielle, at which point my daughter told her how much she missed her. We left feeling like emotional wrecks. We returned home to my flat and comforted each other, sharing the rest of the day together.

My thoughts then began to stray a little to the sense I had that something bad was going to happen. I found myself saying in my mind, *Please, God, let me see in the new year with my father. Don't take him away from me now. I will not be able to cope if you do.*

I tried to put these thoughts completely out of my mind and stay positive because Boxing Day was coming and Gabrielle was still with me at this point. We were still visiting Dad twice a day now. The day was 27 December 2007, and it was time for me to take Gabrielle back to her mother's so she could be with her and her family. I drove her home, told her how much I loved her, thanked her for being there for me, and said to enjoy the rest of the Christmas period.

I returned home and popped down to the cemetery on the way before going to see my dad at hospital. I arrived and spent the next few hours of visiting time with my dad. I became concerned about him even more. He seemed to be more subdued, not himself. The nurses told me he had been comfortable most of the day and that they had not long been in to change him and to suction his throat. They told me it would have worn him out a bit and made him tired.

I spoke with my father's consultant and doctor. They told me that they thought it was only a matter of time before my father might pass away. They were trying to forewarn me of something that

I had known for many weeks now but had been too afraid to accept or, come to terms with, or not faced or spoken to anyone. I had been down this path and seen where this journey led, and it was not a happy place. It was a cold, dark, solemn path that led to despair and overwhelming heartache with my mother. Deep down was my sense that something bad and traumatic was going to happen to me again.

I finished speaking with them and returned to be by my father's side, holding his hands while he slept, all the time praying for him to last into the new year. Visiting time was over, and I had to return home. I called my brother and telling him. We spoke for a while about our father's condition and both wished and prayed for him to last a few more days to the new year.

The date was now 29 December 2007 and the time was 9.30 a.m. Only two more days to go and I would have made it to the new year with my father. I began to wonder if God had heard my prayers. I took my dad's dog for a walk with my dog, and they ran wild, enjoying the open fields. However, my mind was still silently on red alert for something bad to happen, but it was only a distant thought. I felt excited that I would be going to visit my father soon, as visiting would soon be approaching.

Walking both dogs back to my flat, only a few yards away from it, I heard my phone ring. I was apprehensive to retrieve it from my pocket. I instantly had this overwhelming feeling that *bad news was going to happen*. I looked at the screen of my phone as I went to answer it. The word *hospital* was flashing before my eyes. I took some large gasps of air and composed myself before answering it. I answered it, and a female nurse's voice at the other end asked me if I was Daniel Osborne. I answered that I was. She told me her name and said that she was ringing me about my father. By the time she had finished saying his name, I was already in my car and setting off to the hospital.

She said to me, 'I think it would be advisable for you to make your way here to be with your father, as his condition has deteriorated and he is really poorly. With a voice trembling, I told her I had already set off and wouldn't be long. I rang my brother Spencer and told him the nature of the phone call, advising him to make his way there as soon as possible.

The journey I took to my father's hospital took me past the first hospital where he was admitted into, as well as where my late mother was admitted. I had to drive past this hospital where I had already gone through so much heartache and lost so much in my life. As I passed by, I had a million different flashing images start to enter my mind, all in slow motion, and I felt overcome by them.

Struggling to drive with these flashing images compounding my mind, I headed to where my father was being cared for. Spencer also arrived, and we made our way through the entrance and towards the ground-floor corridor to where my father was being cared for. We were met upon arriving by the female nurse who'd called me and informed me of my father's condition. She walked us to see the consultant who was the consultant who also cared for my father at the previous hospital where he was first admitted.

We entered the room, and he told us that the condition of our dad had dramatically deteriorated over the course of the morning and to expect the worse. We went to our father's bedside and saw how poorly he had become. We each pulled a chair up and sat down holding his hands. I became overcome with emotion and walked out into the corridor in tears. The reminders and images of my mother and having her pass away in my arms started to intrude my thoughts. The feeling of my soul being torn apart started to overwhelm my brain once again. I told myself to pull myself together. My dad needed me to be strong for him. I made my way back into the room, realising that the bad thing that I was dreading for months was about to happen.

My brother and I held our dad's hands and told him how much we loved him. When we saw that all was not good, we buzzed for assistance from the doctors or nurses to come, but they came too late. Our beloved father, Ronnie Osborne, age 85, passed away in our arms. Both beside ourselves, we witnessed the loss of a fantastic, wonderful, caring,, and loving devoted husband, father, and granddad. We both now had to say our final goodbyes to Dad, and we left the room inconsolable. I walked outside soaked in the tears that were pouring from my eyes and shouted out at God, 'Not again! You have taken my father and mother. I have hardly anyone, any family, left!'

I was traumatised once again by having another parent pass away in my arms. I wished for the world to swallow me up and take me as well so I could be with my mother and father and care for them. My brother came out and comforted me as best as he could. We consoled each other before heading back inside to make our way to Father's room. We both held each other in tears and said goodbye to Dad. I gently kissed him on his forehead and whispered to him, 'No more suffering now, Dad. Give my love to Mam. I love you both and will miss you forever and always.' I walked out and let my brother say his own goodbyes.

We walked outside comforting each other, and he suggested to me that I should follow him to his house, which I had never been to. I agreed and followed him. When we arrived there, he broke the news to his wife, who consoled him. I looked upon them comforting each other, and it hit me that I now had no one in my life to comfort me other than my daughter, Gabrielle. I had only her to support me in my pain. I felt completely out of place and on edge.

Unsettled, I told them I had to go, that I needed to be on my own, as I always had been, to cope with the traumas that had destroyed my life. I left them alone and made my way to my auntie Meredith's bungalow to break the devastating news about the loss of my dad, her loving brother.

I arrived at her door and made my way into her living room. She said, 'Hello, what are you doing here?'

I sat down and told my 95-year-old auntie that my dad had just passed away. She said, 'No, not again. Not Ronnie.' I comforted her as we cried in each other's arms.

I had a thought come into my mind while holding her. I was now saying in my head, *Please, God. You have taken nearly all that I have loved and cared for away from me and left me alone with no one. Please don't let anything bad happen to my auntie Meredith.* It was a thought I knew should not have even entered my mind at that moment in time, but as I sat holding my late father's sister, my auntie, I could only think of all I had lost, loved, and cherished my entire life.

I quickly swallowed those thoughts and began to console my auntie. After many hours of comforting one another, I had to leave. I made my way straight to the cemetery to be at my mother's side. I collapsed in tears at her headstone and began talking to her, telling her that I had just had Dad pass away in my arms, as she did, and that I now had nothing left of my family other than my daughter and my aunt. I told her, 'You and Dad are together once more. I am so lost without you both. How will I cope at the loss of losing you both in such a short time?'

After an hour or two of being alone with only my thoughts for comfort, I picked myself up off the ground and made my way to my car. Once back at my flat, I knew that I now had to make the phone call to my daughter and once more find the words and the strength to tell her that now she'd lost her grandad, whom she'd doted on all her life. I rang her and informed her once again she had lost another loved one, that I now had lost my mam and dad. As before, she broke down in tears. We spoke for a long time, offering comfort as best we could. Then she put her phone down and her mother consoled her.

Now left alone wandering around the rooms of my flat, I collapsed yet again to my knees and tried to make sense of what was going on. Why were bad things happening to me? What had I done to deserve all this heartache and trauma. I felt as if I were going insane and losing the plot. Am I a bad person to have to suffer all this? Why is this happening to me?

I cried myself to sleep and woke during the night screaming and soaked in sweat. I was tense and shivering. I had just had a truly dreadful nightmare. I was frightened and an emotional wreck. I stayed awake until morning came.

I went to see my doctor, and she gave me a different antidepressant to try to help calm me. She asked how I would cope. I replied that I didn't know, that I felt I was being swallowed up and thrust into the bottom of a dark, soulless well filled with pain, hurt, and sorrow. She told me that she was there if things got any worse and that if I couldn't cope to come straight back to the surgery.

I left the surgery and made my way to my parents' house. I walked in knowing that there was never going to be anyone here for me to take care of or to look after, to hold, to tell them that I loved them. It felt so cold and empty. I couldn't stay there, so I quickly left.

I went to see how Auntie Meredith was coping. Then I had a phone call from my brother Spencer. He told me that the hospital had spoken with him and that he would take care of registering my father's death to save me going through it all. I thanked him and told him that I was with Auntie Meredith. He asked how she was coping. I told him she was OK and that I would look after her.

I then called my other brother, the one who had had something strange happen to him the day that my mother passed away. Ellena answered the phone. I told her that I had lost my father and asked if she would let my brother know. She told me she would when she went to the hospital where he was being treated. She could shed no further light on the subject. When I asked her if she knew what had happened to my brother on the day I lost my mother, she said that the police and doctors told her they had no ideas as to how or why he was found wandering the streets of Holland with no belongings or any ID with him.

She told me she was sorry for my loss and that she would tell my brother. Ellena then asked when the funeral would take place. I said I was not sure yet, that it was too early for that and that I would let her know as soon as I could. We said our goodbyes and hung up.

New Year's Eve came, and I was truly terrified of the prospect of it being my first ever beginning of a new year after I had lost both my parents. I had no hopes, other than thinking that more bad things lay ahead of me in 2008.

New Year's Day came. I stayed in my flat on my own, reflecting on what had gone beforehand, and I got a phone call from my brother Spencer, saying happy New Year, for what it was worth. I said the same back, and he informed me that the date for my father's funeral was going to be 7 January 2008. *What a way to start a new year,* I told myself.

The service was at the same church as my mother's service, held by the same minister, and there would be the same funeral parlour. The church was fifty yards from the family home, and my father was to be laid to rest by my mother's side in our local cemetery. I told my brother thanks for letting me know and that I would let Auntie Meredith know.

I told him I would ring Ellena to let her know. He had the same thoughts as I, and to be honest, we really did not want him over for the funeral, as he had never bothered with my mam and dad for most of his life. I said to my brother spencer that our older brother had had an accident on the day we lost our mam and that he was no threat to spoil the funeral due to his childlike behaviour since his accident or whatever had happened to him. I explained that Ellena told me to look at him and to speak with him, that all was normal, but if you gave him, for instance, a bar of chocolate, he would hold on to it like a child and would be unwilling to let go of it or share it. To be honest, I was apprehensive about seeing him like this.

So we both agreed that if Ellena was coming over and bringing my brother and their three children, whom my parents never really knew, for the funeral, that it was OK and would pass without any incidents, as there had been a life of animosity from me towards our brother.

The day of my father's funeral arrived arrive, and I was feeling lost. It was all too familiar and too soon after losing my mother. Ellena was there with my brother and their children. I saw my brother for the first time since he was last over when he visited my mother in hospital. It was strange to see him. He looked the same and sounded the same, as if there was no difference, but once I began to take note of how he acted and behaved, it became clear that whatever happened to him on the day of returning off a flight from his villa to Holland on the day my mother passed away, he was now a changed man, like a 58year-old with the mind of a child in many ways, although he knew everything that went on or was being told to him. He just couldn't make sense of it properly.

I couldn't help but think that whatever happened on that day of losing my mother that it was something that could not be explained but somehow was meant to happen for the way he'd abandoned our parents and left the care and difficulties of looking after them both all to me, the youngest of all our late parents' children.

The service was difficult, to say the least, for me to go through. I managed with Gabrielle at my side. Again, the minister was as before with my mother's funeral service. He did my father and the family proud, and it was a befitting service for the wonderful father that we had lost.

When the service ended, I held my daughter for comfort. I couldn't lift my heartbroken face to look at anyone in the church. We all made our way out to the outside of the church, with people offering their words of comfort and support. I was struggling to hold myself together, but I somehow managed. The next part of the journey was now going through my mind.

We needed to proceed to the cemetery to lay my father to rest at my mother's side.

We left the church and took the same journey we had with my mother and arrive at the cemetery. I was travelling with my brother and his wife, Gabrielle, and Auntie Meredith. I supported and aided my auntie to where my father was to be placed to rest. The minister held a service of remembrance and love for my father, and then he was at his final resting place at my mother's side.

I fell to my knees looking at my mother's headstone, breaking down, now knowing that I must have the headstone removed once more to have my dad's name put upon it. I was helped to my feet, by whom I do not remember. Friends and family commented on my mother's beautiful headstone that I had gotten for her, the angel holding a heart and watching over her; it now had to watch over both of my wonderful parents.

The service ended, and my father was now laid to rest beside his loving wife of sixty years, he and Freya reunited once more.

We left the cemetery and made our way to where we'd held the function after our mother's funeral—for family and friends to come together and share their fond memories and stories of my parents. People chatted with each other as the hours passed, but I was of no use to anyone. The only thing I truly recall of this day was I that had my photo taken with my two brothers. I was telling myself that this was the last moment we would ever share together as brothers.

Family and friends returned to their homes, and Ellena set off back to Holland with my brother whom she had been divorced and separated from years earlier along with there children. I returned home to my flat, and Gabrielle travelled home to her mother's. I was now alone in my life, with no one other than Gabrielle, and I had lost everything that I ever known, truly cared for, and loved. I was now a lonely man with no mam and dad there for me and siblings that I had no time for and had never been close to, so I was mostly alone in this world now.

Now devastated and traumatised at the loss of my parents, I asked God once again not to allow any more bad things to happen. I couldn't cope with anything else bad happening to me. What other traumas could befall me? After all, I had been through, I just needed time to grieve for my loss of my mam and dad.

I have now shared two traumas. I hoped God would hear my prayers for no further traumas to destroy and change the course of my life forever. He did not hear my calls for help and let me suffer more traumas, pain, and loss.

CHAPTER 3

TRAUMA 3

The Bike Accident that Could Have Killed Me
29 July 2008

After my father was laid to rest at my mother's side, the heartache and bad times began once more. I called into the home where I was raised to feel close to what I had known and lost. It had been full of wonderful memories and happy times that I had shared with my late mother and father. Wandering the coldness of my family home, each room I walked into filled my heart with pain at what I had lost. There were memories and images. The sounds that I heard were ringing from each hollow room that I walked into. I started to have flashing images of the life that I had lived in this home. I saw my mother seated in her chair, and as I glanced towards my father's chair, he was seated there. I heard the TV on as they chatted with each other. My brain was so overtaken with the images and flashing reminders of my mam and dad that I left the house.

A couple of weeks had now passed, struggling to cope and with no support or real comfort other than what family members were still alive, with no support from anyone but my auntie and daughter. I received a phone call from my brother. He said that we should start to think about getting Mam and Dad's house emptied and put on the market. I'd left work to look after for so much of my life, but my life has fallen apart and he was now mentioning this to me so soon after burying my parents. He made my stomach churn with pain and sorrow. I thought, *Fucking typical. You have never helped me over all the years that I struggled on my own with caring for Mam and Dad. You never once lifted a finger when I pleaded for help with getting home help for Dad as he struggled on his own while Mam was in care home.*

I became angry and told him it was too soon for me to even think about doing such a thing. The thought of emptying my family home of all its memories and belonging of my mam and dad … My heart was already broken to shreds.

Another week or so passed, and I got yet another phone call from him regarding the house, but this time things were even worse. He told me had been up to the house and gone through all of my father's drawers and so forth and that he had sat at home working out my father's bank statements and other money-related things. He said nothing added up then accused me of frauding my father out of money over the course of looking after him while I was out of work!

I screamed down the phone at him, calling him a cheeky bastard. 'How dare you accuse me of such a thing!' I told him that I now knew where he lived after the day of losing my dad and that I would be there in five minutes, saying that I was going to kill him. I had lost everything and given so much love and care for my mam and dad that if they could hear him speak this way, they would be utterly disgusted by his words and actions.

Fuck it. I had nothing left in this the world. I drove as fast as I could towards where the piece of shit lived. I had a baseball bat in my car, ready to crack his body to bits. I was enraged with hate. My phone rang again on the way, and I again told the bastard that I was on my way with a baseball bat and that I was going to kill him. 'I'll be five minutes!' I gave him no time even to speak a word, as I was screaming at him so loudly.

I put my phone down and then slammed my brakes on in the middle of the dual carriageway. I rang my doctor and told her what I was about to do. She talked with me, as she was very close to my mother and father for many years while they were poorly. She told me, 'This is not the way your mam and dad would want you to end up doing things.' She told me to come straight home to my flat and that she would meet me there. I agreed, turning around and making my way home, where I meet my doctor and she gave me a sedative to calm me down and knock me to sleep.

To this day, brother, if you ever read this, I will say this to you: If it were not for my doctor and her making me come to my senses over my actions towards what I was going to inflict upon you, you wouldn't be here to read this. Our mother and father would turn in their graves at what you accused me of. If I had continued on my journey to your house … You are lucky to be alive and well today. You even tortured our poor old auntie Meredith with your accusations over this matter, and I tell you and my other brother and sisters that for the way you have all acted over the years towards our mother and father, abandoning them in the manner that you did, you all can rot in hell.

For the five years that Mother was in the care home, each day, twice a day, I would take our father to see his wife. Every time I looked at the visitor signing in book, I hardly ever saw your name there. I'd sit down with Mam and Dad, asking if you had been to see them. Did you even ring them? I leave these words for you to swallow.

They were going to remove you from their will as they did with our other siblings. You could have done more, and you should have taken our mother to your wedding reception, as it broke her heart. You disappointed both Mam and Dad in not making the effort to have them both there for it. I was the one who had to make the excuses for you. You and your wife should be disgusted with yourselves.

Things moved on for a few months. I passed the family home, which had now become an empty shell as it was emptied. I removed all the precious things that I'd held close to my heart, and the house went on the market.

I started to work away again for a while to take my mind away from everything that had happened in my life. I was working with my close friends who had been there to support me through all that I had suffered. They tried to keep things normal for me and were always there if I needed their support or a shoulder to cry on. They knew more about my life than any of my brothers or sisters could ever know. In fact, I always looked upon them as family.

As I was working, my auntie Meredith was coping well, and I had plenty of support for her. A close friend of ten years was like a rock for support, and she helped do my auntie's shopping, paying her bills, and so forth. I only worked away to keep my sanity, as deep in my mind I always wanted to be at home looking after my auntie and being close at hand. I was also longing to go to the cemetery every day. I worked away from March until the middle of July but returned when there was no work. Therefore, I was still home rather often to see to matters, including my daughter, Auntie Meredith, and visiting the cemetery.

I was home midway through the month of July 2008, as it was approaching the first anniversary of losing my mother. While I was home, I arranged for my mother's headstone to be removed and to have my father's inscription and details put on it. It was supposed to be done and replaced before 3 August, the first anniversary of the loss of my mother.

That was the only important thing on my mind at that time, having it replaced so the angel was in place to watch over both my parents. It was a very important day.

During the months leading up to this day, I had not done a great deal of work or earned much, as I was home a lot of the time. I had applied for a grant from the DWP for funds towards finishing paying off the remaining costs of getting the headstone replaced on the correct date in time for the first anniversary of my mother's passing. It was now 29 July and only four days away. I was on edge and anxious, not looking forward to the coming day, and still there was no reply from DWP regarding the funds. I had asked for the help in getting the headstone finished, and if the balance wasn't paid in full it, would not be installed in time.

I got my mountain bike out and decided to go for a ride, as it was a nice warm summer day. I had been a keen cyclist since the day I could ride a bike at the age of 6. I put on my armbands and helmet, bringing along other accessories. I switched my iPod music player on and placed it in my armband. I put my music on to shuffle. I then got on my bike and set off. The time was now 10 a.m. on 29 July 2008. I head towards a local mountain range. At this point, I was working out the journey in my head as to where I was going to ride, all the time in my mind hoping that when I returned home, there would be a letter from DWP awaiting me, saying they had accepted my application for funds.

My journey now planned out in my head, I began my journey whilst listening to my music. I rode up a steep inclined road and down the other side. I then turned right toward a quiet road. I took a left turn and headed towards an old abandoned hospital. The next left, which takes you on a five- or maybe six-mile road, led towards a picturesque small village. I followed this road, and it took me about twenty-five minutes. Then I followed the roads that take you into the village centre. It's not the biggest of places, and it's also where my good friend was working in a hair and massage parlour salon for men. I popped in to see her at work. I had a drink there. I told her I was out to clear my head, as it was Mam's anniversary in a few days and I was on edge, hoping to get the funds together to pay the stonemasons in full for the headstone to be replaced on 2 August 2008 so it was in place for the first anniversary of my mother's passing.

After chatting for a while, I went for a walk along a stream that runs through the village. I found myself buying a loaf of bread to feed the ducks. I went back for my bike from the salon and said goodbye to my friend and her boss. I started to head home, sticking to the route I'd planned. I came back along the five- or six-mile road which I took upon coming into the village. Turning off this road and following some quiet country roads brings you to a place called Ryhope Peak Village. I stopped there and had an ice cream from a shop there. I then climbed back on my bike and continued the return journey home. This part of the journey took me past a local landscape in the area called Rosendale Topping. I spent five minutes looking at the landscape.

Keeping to my route home, I now passed through a place called Birkenfell and then onto the main road back towards home. I rode my bike up this, went down the other side, and headed towards my flat a journey that took at least four hours, taking my time and enjoying the bike ride.

When I reached my flat, I pulled my bike in. Looking on the floor, I saw that there was a letter. I knew it had to be the one I had been waiting for from DWP. I instantly began to feel relieved, thinking that I had been granted what I asked for and would get the headstone replaced in time for my mam's anniversary. Opening the envelope, it revealed a different story and said it was not an appropriate thing to apply for and that they had refused my application.

I became enraged and put the letter in the back pocket of the shorts I was wearing. I decided to go to my local DWP office for an explanation. This was just down the road from where I lived, so I jumped back onto my bike, leaving my helmet in the flat, as it was only a short distance away, less than five minutes on my bike. I locked my door and started cycling back along a stretch of road the other direction from my earlier journey. I headed down a fairly long stretch of road that had a good declining angle to it. I put my bike gears in high speed and started to cycle as fast as I could going downhill. I kept picking up speed.

There was a wide T-junction where you could turn left. I had the right of way, as I was coming downhill on a straight road. No traffic should turn out of this junction and into my path. At this point, I must have easily been going over thirty-five or forty miles per hour downhill on this steep declining road. I started to cross the entrance of this large T-junction. There were many mothers and children on the pavement. I saw a traffic warden ahead of me and other people walking on other pavements, but I was still going full speed.

As I got halfway across this T-junction, I saw a silver Ford Ka approaching the junction and coming up the road from where I was heading. The driver approached this junction, which I was crossing on my bike with no safety helmet, and she turned into the junction on the wrong side to cut the corner to save time on her journey. She cut the corner so aggressively and so fast whilst mounting the pavement, in doing so heading towards parents with their children walking home from school.

When she turned, I didn't have any time to even release my hands and apply them to the brakes, and I smashed full force, travelling thirty-five to forty miles per hour, head-on into the car. I was thrown in slow motion from the impact, and I saw myself coming over the front of my bike and spinning violently towards the windscreen of this car. It looked like the pages of a child's flip page book being flicked in slow motion.

I instantly saw a woman with brown shoulder-length hair and looked straight into the eyes of this woman. As I stared into her face, I was thinking that this was the last face I was ever going to see. *She has killed me. I'm not going to survive this because I'm going too fast downhill.* My head, shoulders, and back smashed into the windscreen of the car. It was as if time froze. I could now hear the shattering impact of my body slamming into the windscreen. The horrible noise was deafening and utterly terrifying. I saw, felt, and heard the windscreen shatter and smash into a million pieces from the impact. It happened in a period of about two seconds, yet it seemed so slow to happen.

Smashing into the windscreen, I then heard women and children's screams. In this split second, I was now thinking that this was it, my life was over. I was not going to survive this accident. I saw past images of my life, including my daughter's face. I told myself that I loved her and wondered how she would cope without me in her life.

I smashed onto the roof of the KA, and once again, I could hear the sound of the impact. There was the sound of metal being crushed as my body slammed into it. I could still hear the sounds of women and children and other people screaming.

I could now feel myself being thrown from the roof of the car, and I began to spin wildly and violently through the air like a rag doll. I felt every turn and every twist that my body was being subjected to, still in slow motion like a flip book. I could see sky then ground, sky then ground, screams upon screams. It seemed to be never ending, and I wondered if it would ever stop. Would I ever land? Would I survive? This was constantly going through my mind.

In the short time it took me to have these thoughts, I was still hearing the screams of surrounding people as my busted rag doll body made its final impact with the tarmac. I again briefly saw the face of the female driver who had ended my life and caused my daughter have no father to watch her grow up.

My body came to a halt, no longer moving, no longer spinning through the air. I heard no more voices, no more screams, no more sounds of windscreens being smashed by my body, no noise of the sound of metal being crushed with my body. I was now lying on the ground, and I began to feel my body seizing up, shutting down. I was unable to move any part of my body. My head fell in the direction of the driver who may have just ended my life. I mustered the breath within my lungs and screamed, 'What the fuck have you done, you stupid fucking bitch! You've killed me!'

Now with no feeling in my body and shouting what may have been my last ever words on this planet alive, my head fell to the other side. I was now looking away from the bedlam of the accident. I saw myself lying in a coffin looking towards my mother and father. I saw their loving faces once more and said with a soft voice, 'I'm here now once more to look after you both and to take care of you.' I felt at peace at this point as I looked upon their faces.

I saw my daughter's face flash before my eyes. I could see the sorrow she was suffering, and I tried telling her how much I love her, how much I would miss her, and that I would always watch over her. Looking back at my mam and dad, I heard their voices one last time. They were both saying the same words to me: 'Son, it is not your time yet. We are not ready for you. You will survive. We are

OK. We have each other once more and are together again. You have your whole life ahead of you with Gabrielle. We will all ways watch over you and Gabrielle. Son, we love you so much.'

I then began to hear other voices. I opened my eyes and was blinded at first by the reflection of the clear blue sky. I then focussed my eyes properly and saw that I was surrounded by dozens of faces that had come to my aid. People were asking, 'Are you OK, mate?' I answered that I didn't know.

I then heard the voice of a man who had witnessed what had happened to me: 'There has been an accident, you bloody idiot.' At this point, a four-by-four suv turned the corner into my path. The man shouting jumped in front of the vehicle, which was close to running over my head, and diverted him around past me

I was thinking that if the driver of the car hadn't killed me, he sure as hell nearly did. I recognised a young lad who lived near me asking, 'Are you OK, mate?' I said I wasn't.

I now heard people screaming at the driver angrily. I heard someone say, 'Someone phone for an ambulance and police!'

I found myself looking through the crowd of people that now surrounded me, and I saw the face of the driver standing there looking over the damage to her car. I shouted more abuse towards her and then she tries to do something that to this day still confounds me. She tried to get into her car to move it to the correct side of the junction, which she should have taken in the first place and allowed me to pass safely, as I had the right of way with going straight ahead. People stopped her from moving her car.

As I looked on in amazement at her actions, I then realised just where I was, how far I was away from impacting her car. I was about twenty to twenty-five feet away and lying on the side of the junction where she should have correctly turned.

I shouted once more, 'You stupid cow! It's too late for that. Look what you have done to me!' My body was in shock and unable to move.

I then heard the sounds of sirens in the distance as I lay on the ground. I had intrusive disturbing reminders of all that I had gone through in the past with ambulances. I began to see their lights and hear their sirens in my mind.

I then heard the sirens and saw the flashing blue lights from the ambulance that had been called to help me. I saw it pull up next to my busted body, and the paramedics got out and came towards me. I instantly got upset and scared, filled with fear as I saw the faces of the paramedics. They were the ones who were called when I rang for an ambulance for my father the day he had a stroke in my arms.

They began to ask me questions and examine me. I heard people shouting and venting their anger towards the driver of the Ford KA. I also saw the driver of the car and heard children crying and being comforted by their parents as to what they had just witnessed.

The paramedics rolled my body onto a stretcher and put a neck brace around my throat and around my spine. That's when I heard more sirens and saw more flashing blue lights pull up. The police had just arrived. I heard them ask the paramedics about my condition. They told the police that they must get me straight to hospital. I started to be overcome with everything. I was now ruminating on the intrusive flashing images of being taken to the same A&E were I had so many bad things happen regarding my mam and dad.

They started on their journey from the scene. I wasn't sure if I was going to lose my life and was still unsure if I was going to survive while I was in the ambulance. The paramedics started putting needles into my arms to put a drip up and administer painkillers. As they set off from the scene of my accident, the journey became all too familiar. It became apparent that we are taking the exact same route that my mam and dad had travelled on their journey to the same hospital, the same A&E that I was being taken to.

I recall saying to the paramedic treating me in the back of the ambulance, 'You were the one who attended to my father's home last September.' I then told him that whatever was wrong with me to get me fixed up and sent home, as I couldn't afford to stay in hospital, no matter what was up with me, as I had to get my mother and father's headstone being installed in four days, ready for the first anniversary of my mam passing away.

He looked into my eyes and told me that I had just been in a head-on car accident. 'You were on a bike. After seeing the state you're in, you won't be leaving the hospital in a hurry.'

I told him, 'I can't stay in hospital. I hate the place. I have suffered too much loss and heartache there. You just watch me. I won't be staying anywhere.'

The paramedic looked down at me and laughed, saying, 'Trust me—you will be in hospital for a while.'

When we arrived at the hospital A&E where my parents were admitted, I was rushed in, passing the way my late parents were taken into the same ward of A&E. I began panicking now, thinking of past times, and then the images of late start to come to mind. I thought, *For God's sake, I hope they don't put me in the same cubicle that either my mam or dad were put in when they were brought here.*

Yet I was placed in the same cubicle my mother was in when she was taken to hospital a year ago. My brain went into overdrive. I became so overcome with the trauma of this being the same cubicle that I passed out. When I came around, I heard many voices surrounding me. I heard the paramedics telling the doctors my name and the nature of my accident. At this point, there must have between eight and ten doctors and nurses in the cubicles surrounding me. I could now see and hear the cubicle curtains being drawn closed. I began to feel shut in in the confined space with the bedlam of it all.

They then lifted the stretcher I was strapped to and placed me onto a bed, still attached and strapped to the stretcher. They wrapped me in sheets, and the paramedic turned to me and got my attention. He said, 'I picked your phone up at the scene of the accident. Is there anyone you want me to inform?'

I paused before I answer If he was wanting to inform my next of kin, things looked bad for me. Panicking with this in my mind, I asked myself whom I should inform. I had only Gabrielle and my aunty Meredith, I couldn't let them do that how would they of taken that phone call but I give them Gabrielle's details and they go to make the call to Gabrielle in fear for how she would of reacted to such horrendous news panic set in. He went out to make a call but then returned, saying there was no answer. I told him to keep trying or try another person from my phone book who could possibly get hold of Gabrielle.

My attention then focused on my surroundings, and I saw images of being in the same cubicle with my mam. This terrified me. I started shouting, 'Get me out of here! My mam was in this cubicle!'

The doctors began to focus on me with the nurses after finding out what had happened to me from the paramedics. They asked, 'Are you OK? Where is the pain? Can you tell us what has happened?'

Terrified, confused, and in shock, I told the doctors surrounding me that I didn't know where it hurt. I couldn't feel any part of my body. As I told him, I now saw flashing images of scenes from programs like *Casualty*, where there had been some kind of accident and all the doctors and nurses struggled to keep someone alive. This was the reality of the trauma I was actually going through in the hospital *now*.

I was examined and then rushed for an MRI scan. I was overcome once again with panic, as I had had MRI scans before for problems with my back. Therefore, I knew what to expect. The thought of going for an MRI scan now set in, and I became so upset and traumatised at the thought of it that I think I passed out. The next thing I recall is opening my eyes to find that I was inside the MRI scat scan machine. In the past when I had MRI scans done, it took a long time because I suffer from claustrophobia. I am afraid of confined spaces, and the inside of an MRI scan machine is like being placed inside a coffin with restricted movement. I truly am frightened of the machine.

But this time while I was in the machine getting scanned, I was unable to move or fidget about because I was still strapped to the stretcher and unable to move any body part other than to scream and shout in tears. I heard a voice through a built-in speaker inside the scan machine telling me to relax and close my eyes. I tried doing this, but the rumbling, vibrating extreme loud noise that the machine makes when it is functioning is a truly horrific noise. I screamed for it to be over, but I was stuck in it and petrified. I felt as I were trapped inside a coffin unable to move. It felt as I were buried alive.

I was in the MRI machine for what felt like hours. The machine finally slid me outwards and away from the noises. The machine fell silent as my head finally emerged from the machine. *Thank God that's over,* I thought. But I had no time to relax or breathe a sigh of relief because I was rushed to another room for a brain scan. Panic once again took over, and I was traumatised further with this.

After the two scans, I was then rushed into the X-ray room for a set of full body X-rays to be done on me—and just after already being traumatised with the MRI scan. *Brain scan? What the fuck is up with me? What has the woman done to me? Am I going to survive this? And if I do, what damage is done to me? Will I ever walk again or will I be in a wheelchair for the rest of my life?* If I was going to be in a wheelchair, I wished she'd just killed me outright.

I was in the X-ray room for about forty minutes or so and was then taken back to the cubicle. I was admitted to the one with so many bad memories and was once again surrounded by doctors and nurses running around my stretched out body. I saw them looking at X-ray results, talking with each other about the results while they waited to hear about my MRI scan results. They decided they needed further X-rays. I asked myself again, *What state am I in? What has this woman done to me?*

Then I was rushed to another room for an ultrasound scan, my fourth scan since arriving to hospital. I was thinking, *There is no way I will be getting out of hospital in a hurry. I won't be home in three days to have the headstone replaced with my father's name placed on it next to my mother's.*

I became angry and frustrated. I shouted, 'You fucking bitch, look at what you have done to me.

Who's going to make sure I have the headstone replaced in time for the first anniversary of losing my mam!'

I was crying uncontrollably getting the fourth scan done. The nurse doing the scan talked to me, and I told her, 'I don't care what is up with me. I can't be staying in hospital. I have to be out of here. I have something important that I have to do in less than four days.' She said the same thing as the paramedic, that I was in no fit state to be going anywhere, not for a long time.'

I told her, 'Just you watch me. I will not be staying here—the only way I will is if I die.' I told her that it was too important for me to miss and that I was the only person to take care of it, that I had no family to do it. I added that I never let my parents down when they were alive and that I was not about to start now.

This thought stayed with me during the time I was having my fourth scan. Once it was finished, I was once more wheeled back to my cubicle. Doctors and nurses were surrounding me as before, telling me why I had so many scans and X-rays. They were telling me that there could be a chance of brain damage from the impact of hitting a car at the speed I was doing on my bike with no helmet on.

They were in and out of my cubicle for about an hour. They returned and told me they wanted to take me back in for another MRI scan. I was already traumatised with all that had happened to me with the first scan and the others. The panic hit once more when they started wheeling my battered and busted body back along the corridors towards the MRI room. Besides myself, I tried to prepare myself once more for what I was about to go through.

I was still strapped to the stretcher I was placed on at scene of the accident. I lay on the sliding bed of the MRI machine and at once I felt the sliding drawer pull me onto the machine. I heard the operator's voice telling me to try to keep still (who was she kidding?). I had not been able to move my body for at least three hours; the only thing I could move were my eyes. I squeeze them closed as tightly as I could, and then the machine started up once more.

The noise was again terrifying and traumatising. The feeling of been in a coffin struck once more. This time inside it seemed to take longer, and I had time to reflect on just what had happened to me and the severity of it all. I wished for this to hurry and be over, but it felt like an eternity. Finally, my second MRI was over and I was yet again returned to the dreaded cubicle.

I was again surrounded by the sight of doctors and nurses. They were in and out over the next hour, and I was finding things hard to understand. Left on my own, unable to move or make sense of everything, all I could think about was my mother. I saw the reminding images of that day and became teary-eyed. I was overwhelmed with my emotions in the empty cubicle.

Suddenly, I heard the soft voice of a female nurse who had entered the cubicle. She asked, 'Are you OK there? Are you bleeding?'

I told her I had no idea, that I couldn't really feel my body. She went to get the attention of the doctors and nurses by hitting the red panic button. The cubicle was once again filled with their presence, and it became a chaotic scene again.

Upon the arrival of the doctor's and nurses coming back into my cubicle after the nurse had hit the red emergency button it became clear why she pressed it as when she looked in and asked if I was ok? It was because she had noticed a pool of blood had formed on the cubicle floor which was not there before and no one knew at this point where the blood was actually coming from but to know that there was now a pool of blood frightened me and I was now I even more afraid and scared for my life.

I was now terrified and panicking, frightened of losing my life to the bleeding. If there was blood then how bad was I bleeding? It had now been five or six hours since my accident.

The doctors and nurses started to remove the blankets that had covered my body since arriving at the hospital. They began to examine me for open cuts and wounds. They saw nothing at first, but then they said, 'Let's roll Mr Osborne onto his left side.'

I was now thinking, *Oh my God, what if they roll me on my side and my spine is damaged or I have something stuck through me?*

They carefully rolled me onto my side. As they did, I somehow managed to look over my right shoulder. I had been lying in a huge pile of blood. It covered my entire body and filled the stretcher I was brought to the hospital in. There was such a large amount of blood. I instantly screamed as panic and sheer fear took hold of me. I shouted, 'I'm bleeding to death! What's up with me? Where is all this blood coming from?'

They began to wipe my body with some towels and placed the towels on the stretcher to soak up all the blood. The floor was also covered in towels to soak up my blood. I heard a doctor say, 'Mr Earl, you have a very large abrasion and a hole in your right thigh.'

I manage to see the wound looking over my right shoulder. I couldn't believe it. My right thigh had a very large open cut in it, and I could see deep inside this wound. As the doctor wiped the blood away, I then saw blood coming from a round puncture wound only an inch or so away from the open cut. There was part of the car's aerial imbedded in my thigh. Looking at the damage to my thigh, I felt severe pain in my ribs. I began screaming in utter fear of my life. 'Help me! Please help me. Tell me what's wrong with me! Am I going to die? Someone please tell my daughter, Gabrielle, that I love her and will always watch over her.'

I felt overcome with it all, and I recall passing out. I later came around, and I had been prepared to have my right thigh stitched and repaired. I was given blood, as I had lost so much, and the doctors told me that they needed to give me a sedative to take any pain away in order to relax me. They injected all my open wounds that were bleeding so they could stitch them back together. They gave me a sedative through a drip, which helped relax me slightly. I heard the doctor say, 'This is going to hurt when I inject around the wounds, so brace yourself.'

I felt nothing at first as he injected me about seven or eight times. I could then feel pain in my thigh once the needles were going in. He told me that it was nearly done. I was unable to answer, as I was biting my jaw together so tightly with sheer fear.

The doctor now told me that he was going to start stitching my wounds back together. I braced myself at the thought of it and the pain I would feel from him doing this. As he put the needle in, I thankfully felt nothing. It took half an hour to stitch all my wounds together. He said, 'That's it, Mr Osborne. It's over, all done.' I thanked him as he left the cubicle I had now been in for six hours.

Still lying on the bed in the cubicle, I was informed that they were going to check all the X-rays and scans that I had in order to make sure they were OK. I was again left alone in the cubicle.

I hoped everything was all clear, as I was not staying in here any longer than I had to. My mother's anniversary was only four days away. Who would sort that out if not me?

A doctor showed his face through the cubicle curtains and told me there was a police officer here who would like to speak to me if I was up to it. I said that that was OK.

The officer came in and pulled up a chair, asking me how I was feeling. I said, 'I'm not sure, Officer. I've just been stitched back together and am waiting for doctors to tell me about all the scans I had done to see if there is any damage.'

'Do you feel like you could tell me what happened to you?'

I replied yes and told him everything that had happened in regards to the accident. I said that the woman in question (the driver of the silver KA) could have killed me and that she tried to move her car to the other side of the junction to make it look as if she had done nothing wrong.

The officer told me he was aware of that, but there were too many witnesses and it made no difference. She was completely at fault. He then told me that upon arriving at the scene of the accident that the first officers that attended actually allowed her to move the vehicle to the other side of the junction, which she shouldn't have. He said that there was an accident investigator and that the officers should not have allowed her to move the vehicle, as he didn't know the condition of the man she hit or if he had even survived.

I started to shout at him, saying that she was going to get away with nearly killing me. I didn't understand how the people they were supposed to help allowed her to break the law and get away with this, the *fucking bitch*.

'You don't need to worry about anything, Mr Osborne; the officers that allowed her to move her car will be investigated for their actions. I have several statements from people who witnessed the accident. She will get away with nothing.' He took my statement and then left the hospital.

Fancy the police letting her move her car after what she had done to me. Where was the justice in that?

The doctors returned with the results of my scans. I braced myself for bad news, expecting the worst. Apparently, I had sustained four fractured ribs. The wounds that I had were stitched back together, and everything else appeared to be normal. There were no signs of brain damage. My spine was OK, and they would be keeping me in hospital for a few days for observation.

A doctor told me that I was the luckiest person alive. 'I have never, in all the years of being a doctor, seen a man come into this hospital with the nature of your accident, wearing no helmet and going thirty-five to forty miles per hour downhill on a bike. Then a full head-on crash with a moving car … You truly are a lucky man. Someone somewhere is watching over you.'

I became overwhelmed with emotions. I began to cry, telling him it must have been my mother and father looking out for me and that they wanted me to live longer. 'But if you think that I am staying in hospital for a few days for observation, then you now watch me get out of this cubicle that my mother was in—and this A&E ward where I have had so many bad things happen to me. Watch me get up, stand on my two feet, and go home. I have something important to do that no one other than I can do.'

'What is that, Mr Osborne?'

I told him about the headstone and said that no other family member gave a shit to do it.

'It's a miracle that you have survived this accident, let alone are able to get up and walk out on the same day. As much as I would like to see you do that, which would be a miracle to see, I think you will be in here for at least a few days.' He exited the cubicle.

I told myself that it was time to get out of this bed and stand on my two feet. I didn't have time to stay here. I had no brain damage, and I should be able to walk, as there was no spinal damage.

I mustered all my strength and courage, thinking all the time that I would not let myself down. I would get the headstone in place even if it killed me. I rolled to one side of the bed and placed my feet on the floor. I could feel the coolness of the floor as my two feet touched it. I was not disabled; I had movement. I pulled my battered body to its feet and stood upright. I was wearing nothing but a T-shirt, with all my other lower parts not covered, as they had cut my shorts off to examine me to find out where I was bleeding from.

I hit the buzzer for attention, and the male nurse who thought it was a miracle I survived entered. I told him to watch me get up and leave this hospital. 'I told you I have a headstone to be replaced. I don't have time to stay here.' He looked at me in amazement. 'Do you want me to walk through the wards of this hospital naked or have you something I can wear?'

He went and got me a pair of vile hospital pyjama bottoms and helped me into them. I asked him where the shorts were that I had on when I came here.

'I have no way of getting home from here,' I told him. 'I have no one at all who can pick me up, and I don't fancy walking from here in these awful pyjamas to my flat.'

'I will have to get the doctor to see you to see if he will allow you to leave.'

'Best get him then, mate, as I need to be gone from here. I have too much to do.'

The doctor came in my cubicle and asked, 'What on earth are you doing, Mr Osborne? Where do you think you're going? We need to admit you to a ward so we can observe you for a few days.'

I told him that I was going home and didn't have the time to be staying in here. I really needed to be away from here. I was having too many upsetting flashbacks and reminders of my time spent in this hospital with my late mam and dad.

He told me that he would have to give me a thorough examination and be sure that it was safe for me to be allowed to return home.

Eventually but reluctantly, he allowed me to leave the A&E so I could go home, although he said the same to me as the male nurse had, that it was a miracle that I had survived this kind of accident. 'I am amazed that you were not killed outright, let alone are able to stand and walk after seven hours and well enough to return home.' He told me he would rather I stay for observation for a few days but that he understood my reasons for the urgency in wanting to leave. 'If you feel that you need to return, don't hesitate to phone for an ambulance.'

I laughed and told him I never, ever wanted to be anywhere near this hospital or inside of or near an ambulance for as long as I lived. I was sick of the sight of this hospital and ambulances.

On my way towards the A&E entrance, I passed the paramedic who had brought me here earlier. I said, 'I told you that I would not be staying in here, as I have my parents' headstone to sort out.'

'I'm amazed that you are up and walking so soon. I thought you would be in here for a very long time.' He wished me a quick recovery and said they hoped all was OK for me.

Someone ordered me a taxi, which arrived shortly after, and I made my way—battered and busted, stitched back together, and wearing hospital pyjama bottoms—to the taxi, feeling embarrassed about the bottoms I was wearing. I was helped into the taxi to head home.

The taxi driver helped me to my door, and I made my way into my flat. I managed to get up the stairs, where I sat down on a comfortable leather swivel chair and reflected on the disturbing, terrifying,, and truly traumatic events that I had just gone through.

Alone and totally distraught, I asked myself how on earth I had survived that. Had I not suffered enough in recent times? I once again said to God, 'How many more traumatic things do you wish me to suffer? Will you please stop all these bad things from happening to me. I can't cope with any more bad things happening to me or my family.'

I have now spoken of three of my traumas. But more was to come … and not long after the bike accident. I am now going to tell the story of the final trauma's to befall me: the passing of the last of my family members, my beloved 95-year-old auntie Meredith. And also my best friend Stan the man.

Below are some photos from different angles of the scene of my bike accident. The first picture shows where the Ford KA mounted the pavement and how aggressively the wrong side of the junction was cut. It was on the pavement as it turned into the path of me approaching at thirty-five to forty miles per hour on my mountain bike.

The second picture shows the couple about to cross the T-junction in the direction I was travelling. It also shows a silver BMW four-by-four cutting the same corner of the junction—but not as severely as the Ford KA that cut me up. It shows how other cars didn't turn on the correct side of the junction. It also shows the scale and size of the T-junction.

The third picture shows where my body landed from the impact. The Ford KA that I hit was on the far opposite pavement as it cut the corner in front of me. Count the small white lines of the correct side, which the Ford KA should have turned from. If you look at it as you count to the sixth small single line, you'll see that it shows a light patch on the picture with what looks like wood chippings. This was where I landed after I impacted the driver's car! Some distance, don't you agree?

CHAPTER 4

TRAUMA 4

The Passing of My Auntie Meredith, 95 Years of Age

Feeling distraught and alone in my flat, I sat in my chair and wished for nothing else bad to happen to me or my family. I called Gabrielle to inform her of what had happened to me, telling her that I was involved in an accident whilst out on my bike.

She asked if I was OK. I told her not to worry, that I was home in the flat and that I should be OK. When I told her in detail what happened, she became very upset and said, 'When will everything stop happening to us, Dad?'

I replied, 'I honestly don't know, sweetheart. I am asking myself the same question. I cannot cope with much more; I don't want anything else bad to happen to our family. I have only you and Auntie Meredith left. I don't know what I would do if anything were to happen to either of you.' We chatted for about an hour, and she said she wanted to come down to be with me. I told her that I'd be OK and that if there was any change, I'd let her know. I said not to worry and that I would ring her the next day. We said good night.

After I hung up the phone, I continued to sit in my chair, reliving the traumas I had suffered. I couldn't handle the thought of going to bed and having to close my eyes to go to sleep. I remained sitting in my chair, feeling completely worn, shattered with emotions, and in severe pain, and I fought to stay awake. I was frightened to fall asleep in case I didn't wake up.

I fell asleep from exhaustion but woke up in my chair during the night. I found myself screaming and soaked in sweat. I had seen myself laid out in a coffin with my daughter standing over me saying goodbye to me and telling me how much she loved me. Disturbed at this, I kept myself awake for the rest of the night.

I realised the reason I had awakened screaming and soaked in sweat. I'd had a very detailed and vivid nightmare about the accident and how traumatised I was by everything. I had just gone through. and it scared me so much. It was so disturbing that I wet myself with the fear of it.

It was now the morning after my accident, 30 July 2008, and there were only four days before my mother's first anniversary and only two days before the headstone was due to be replaced, and I still had to find the money to pay the balance off so that it could be installed in time before the anniversary that was looming.

I struggled to put on a pair of loose tracksuit bottoms, as I was in agony. But I somehow managed to dress myself and get ready. I now had the daily task of going to see to my auntie Meredith to assist her. I exited my flat and made my way to my car, but as I tried to get into it to drive to my auntie's, the pain became too unbearable. So I made my way there on foot, which took me about an hour, whereas during a normal walk in good health, it was only five minutes away.

When I arrived at my auntie's bungalow and made my way down the drive, my auntie saw me from her window near the front door. Once I'd entered, I heard my auntie say, 'Is that you? Are you OK?'

I headed to the front living room where she was sitting, thinking, *She is 95 years of age and saw me lose my mother and father only a few months ago. How will she cope seeing me in the state I'm in after the accident? She has seen too much suffering to have this to deal with as well.*

When I approached her, she instantly saw my state and asked, *What is up with you? What's happened now?*

I sat next to her and told her everything that had happened to me. She became so upset with it all. 'It's OK, Auntie Meredith. I'll be fine. I don't want you to worry over it. I don't want you to panic or get upset over it all. I'll still be able to come and look after things and do your errands and such. But it won't be every day, as I am in agony with it.' She settled down after I reassured her that I would be OK.

I went down to the post office to draw her pension and pay a few bills. While I was there, I started to panic and became concerned over the chest pains that I started getting. With my doctor only being a short walk away from the post office, I made my way there and asked to see Dr Janice. She had supported me so much and helped me with all my difficulties with my family. She knew very well the traumas and bad time that I had had to cope with in my life.

I was taken straight in to see her. As I slowly made my way to her room and entered, she said, 'What on earth has happened to you? Look at the state of you.' When I told her what had happened to me, she said that she could not believe it. 'How on earth are you holding things together?'

'I don't know. I am not sure how much more I can cope with, Doctor. I have had enough and can't take any more.'

She asked why I had come to see her. I told her more about the accident, adding, 'Yesterday I was having difficulty breathing properly, and it's hurting when I breathe.'

She said, 'You should have stayed in hospital, where they could have kept an eye on you.' She knew the response I would give her before I had time to say it.

She examined me and told me, 'I think it would be for the best if you were to go back to hospital for them to check you over properly.'

I reluctantly agreed. I was in so much pain that I allowed her to ring for an ambulance to return me to hospital and the A&E yet again.

An ambulance arrived to the surgery to transport me, and I started to ask myself what could be wrong with me. I was given the all-clear yesterday, and there was no serious damage to me. I arrived and was taken into the A&E. I instantly felt anxious and overcome at my return here.

I will keep it short at this point, as I don't want to drag it out. The outcome was that they took further scans and X-rays to make sure everything was fine. They said it was and that the pain I was suffering was due to my broken ribs, which they said would take time to heal on their own.

Given the news, I returned to my flat by taxi. I began thinking about getting the balance of the headstone paid off in full so it could be installed on 2 August 2008.

A day before the anniversary, I managed to pull it off by selling a few belongings. I made my way to the stonemasons and paid off the balance. The woman told me that the headstone would be put back in the place where I now wanted it, which was in between my mam and dad so it looked central and the angel on headstone would look over both my parents. She gave me a time to meet the stonemasons at the cemetery on so I could be there for its installation.

They could only install the headstone and not the corner pieces and plinths, as they were not allowed to do so. It was up to me to install and cement them in place. Knowing I would not be able to lift the plinths and level them out set in concrete, I asked a close friend of mine for help in installing the plinths and setting them right.

It was finally completed and was ready for me to be able to take my remembrance wreaths down for my mother's anniversary the day after. Below is a photo of the headstone placed over my mother and father.

Without the help of my good friend, I would not have been able to manage putting it into place. I thanked him for all of his help and support; it truly meant a lot to me. So this is what I struggled with: a busted and battered black-and-blue body. But I managed to have it replaced in time for the anniversary, and this is the reason I could not waste any time in hospital, as there was no one else who was going to do this.

Having this installed in time was what drove me on while I was in hospital. I'd told everyone from the paramedics to the nurses and doctors that I would walk out of that hospital and get this headstone installed in time, even if it killed me.

Now that the headstone was installed and looked beautiful, I took wreaths down from my daughter and me, also from my auntie Meredith, and placed them upon their graveside, hoping that they were looking down on me to give me the strength to survive the pain I was going through from my accident and that nothing else bad was to happen to me. I hoped I had made them proud of me and what I had done for them, especially under the circumstances of what I had just been through.

Emotionally done in and physically battered, the day had worn me out. I went home to be alone with only my thoughts for comfort and rested my broken body, allowing myself to break down from the stress of all I had suffered.

The days began to pass slowly, and my body began the long process of healing itself, while I was trying my best to keep myself together so I could be strong enough to look after the last one of the only remaining family members I had left from my side of the family, my auntie Meredith other than my auntie Meredith the only other family I had to care for and be there for was my daughter Gabrielle . I also needed to try to concentrate on my brother pushing the sale of the family home through so he could have his inheritance. He was also going on to my elderly auntie with his accusations of my frauding my beloved father out of money. He was nothing more than a selfish human being who was probably feeling guilty over the years for never showing any empathy, compassion, or thought for anyone else other than his own needs.

My auntie told me she was sick of him calling her. She told me that she'd told him to stop ringing her over it, as she knew far too well that there was no truth in it and she knew that I had given so much of my life to care for my parents as well as her. She told him off over it, as she was enraged and upset with his attitude towards it all.

I rang my cold-hearted so-called brother Spencer and told him that if I had not nearly just lost my life and could make my way to his home that I would beat the daylights out of him. I called him a waste of time and told him to rot in hell with the rest of my brothers and sisters, adding that if he continued to upset my aunt Meredith at her age, he'd better watch his back.

One week passed, and it was 10 August 2008, only two weeks after my accident and having my parents' headstone replaced. I received a phone call from my aunt May's hairdresser, Jane, who went round to my aunt's to cut and curl her hair. She had rung me to tell me that she was there doing her hair and that my auntie was not well. She asked if I could come down.

I told her I was on my way and wouldn't be long. I walked down, as it was still extremely difficult to drive my car. When I arrived to my auntie Meredith's, I went straight into her home and began to talk to the hairdresser. I got as much information from her as possible, upon which I then made my way into the living room. I could instantly see that my auntie did not look well. I now had to make the decision to call for the doctor to come out to see to her.

I now sat comforting my auntie, and we waited for the arrival of the doctor, who eventually turned up. He did a thorough examination of her and advised me that he thought it would be best to call for an ambulance to take her to hospital, the same hospital that I had spent so much time in lately. I told Jane in the kitchen that I couldn't believe my luck and that I could not cope with this and returning to the same hospital with one of my last remaining family members.

'I will come with you to the hospital to support you,' she said.

'Thank you,' I said. 'If it's not too much trouble for you, then I would really appreciate that, as I have gone through so much recently and am not sure how I will cope in having to go back to the same hospital so soon.'

The ambulance arrived to my auntie's bungalow. I couldn't believe my misfortune. It turned out to be the same ambulance with the same paramedics who attended to the scene of my bike accident only two weeks earlier. I was overcome with it all, and I started getting flashing images of the recent traumas only a short time ago. My mind was being bombarded with these intrusive images, disturbing reminders, and the harrowing nerve-rending feelings of reliving my accident and all the other traumas that I had gone through again.

The paramedics entered my auntie's bungalow and began to assess her condition while I stood in the kitchen a nervous wreck at the very sights and sounds of the ambulance and paramedics.

Jane came in and chatted with me for a short while, until the paramedics asked me to go into the living room. I apprehensively approached the room, expecting to hear what I was not wishing to hear, and they informed me that they would have to take my auntie Meredith to hospital. Hearing those words and knowing what lay ahead of me, I became overcome. But I showed no emotions in front of my auntie. I had to be strong and supportive of her needs now. I told them that I would follow them as they took my auntie to hospital.

Jane told me that she would drive me in her car behind the ambulance so that I was spared the discomfort of having to travel in the same ambulance that I had had so many bad experiences with in the last year of my life.

I thanked her for doing this, and we started following the ambulance. I told Jane of my recent time spent in hospital and that I was dreading the thought of going back there and through A&E once more. She could tell by my voice how anxious I was of this and offered to stay with me while my auntie was admitted, which I thought was a huge support for me.

The ambulance was now taking us on the *exact same journey*, road for road, that my mother was taken on when she went to hospital. It was also the exact same journey that my father had taken and the exact same journey that I was taken on only two weeks earlier. I turned to Jane and told her that I didn't fucking believe my luck. How could it be possible to have this amount of bad luck in less than a year? My mother, my father, myself, and now my auntie, all in the same ambulance and all going the exact same route to the exact same hospital in the exact same A&E. How could life possibly get any worse for me!

Hearing what I had just told her, she said she would come into the hospital to support me through going back in there so soon. Once again, I told her how grateful I was for her support and said that

I just hoped to God that my auntie was not taken into the same cubicle that my mother and I were admitted into. 'How bad would that be?' I told her.

'I know,' she replied. 'That would be awful for you. There are plenty of other cubicles in the A&E ward that she could be taken into. Don't worry. That surely won't happen.'

As Auntie Meredith was wheeled into the A&E reception and her details were taken from the receptionist, she had a look of bewilderment on her face as she took the details down; she had recognised me from a few weeks prior when I was admitted after my bike accident.

Auntie Meredith was then taken down to where the cubicles were, which at this point were out of my line of sight. One paramedic wheeled her down while I was asked by the other to help assist with completing the rest of booking her in at the reception desk. I gave them details of her age, address, and so forth. While doing this, the reminders and images of doing this with both my mother and father flashed before my eyes. If felt like only yesterday that I had done this for them both.

With a trembling voice and still in shock at once again being in this place, I answered the receptionist's questions regarding my auntie.

After answering all the questions, I was asked to take a seat.

I said, 'If it's OK, I'll stand, as I am still in agony from the injuries from a bike accident I had two weeks ago.' I was still getting flashing images and reminders of the past traumas I had encountered at this hospital. I walked outside to take some deep breaths of fresh air to help compose myself, knowing that I was going to be asked to go through to the cubicle area where my auntie was being looked at.

Now on edge with my brain switching to red alert for further distressing bad news, I heard Jane calling out my name. 'Daniel, they're asking for you to go down to see the doctors in the cubicle area.'

I took two more deep breaths for composure and entered the A&E ward. I followed Jane down towards where I was now dreading to look. I began to shake and go dizzy, with arms and legs feeling unstable, but I just looked towards the floor, telling myself one thing: *Please, for God's sake, don't take me into the same cubicle where I spent so much time in pain, heartache, and suffering.*

I saw all the familiar faces of the past as if I knew them personally from bad times. I saw a doctor walk towards me. He had a strange look come over his face. I greeted him by saying, 'I am sick of coming here and seeing your face!'

He said, 'What are you doing back here so soon? You were only in here a week or so ago. I was the doctor who saw you, wasn't I?'

'Yes. I hope you have good news for me about my auntie Meredith. I hope she's not in the same cubicle that I was in … Is she?'

The look on this doctor's face was a confounded one. A look of being lost for words was etched over his face. He told me to follow him and said that he would take me to see her. I followed him, all the while praying it not going to be the same cubicle where I thought I was going to lose my life.

As I followed the doctor, he began to head towards the left-hand side cubicles. My heart rate soared, my breathing became ever so more erratic, and intrusive flashing vivid images started to flash before my eyes faster and faster. My heart was once more racing in my chest, and I had thoughts of *Please don't have my auntie in the place*, but it was to no avail.

I was speechless when I was shown into the very same cubicle where I had spent so many bad times. I could not believe my luck. How could this be possible? How much misfortune did I have to suffer in this hospital? I was once more devastated and traumatised. I asked for help sitting down as I became ever more stressed out and agitated, confused, and in shock with it all.

I was still accompanied by Jane, and I tried to pull myself together enough so that I could ask my auntie Meredith how she was feeling. She said, 'I'm OK. I shouldn't be in here. I don't know what all the fuss is about.'

'It's for the best, Auntie Meredith, so we can find out what's wrong with you.'

'Take me home,' she said. 'I don't want to be in here. I want to be at home. I don't know what all the fuss is over.'

'You'll be home before you know it, Auntie. Don't worry—I will keep an eye on your house. You just let the doctors find out what's wrong with you so we can get you better and back home.'

After about an hour or so of sitting with her and keeping her company, the doctor I now knew far too well put his head into the cubicle and asked if he could speak with me in private. I said yes. Jane sat with my auntie to keep her company.

I managed to lift myself to my feet and tell my auntie that I wouldn't be long, that I was just going to the toilet.

I followed the doctor into a room where he told me he would be sending my auntie Meredith to a ward in the hospital for them to assess her condition to try to find out what was wrong with her. I hoped to God that they would not say the name of any wards that I had shared with lost loved ones.

He then destroyed my world yet again by telling me he would be admitting my auntie Meredith to ward 5. I couldn't make sense of his words at first. I heard them, but all I could see in my head were flashing images of holding my mother in my arms and her passing away in my arms. I saw her face and could remember telling her how much I loved her as if had just happened yesterday. I broke down, inconsolable and in agony and with floods of tears pouring down my face. I pled for help from God. Why me? What had I done to deserve so much suffering?

The doctor went and got some help, and I was helped into the seat in his room, where I was comforted by a female nurse I also recognised from my times spent there. She sat with me for a while, long enough for me to find the strength to pull myself together to return to be at my auntie's bedside.

I went back into the cubicle to sit for a while whilst we waited for her to be taken to ward 5. I went and got a drink of water with Janet and told her what the doctors told me as to where they were going to take my auntie. She was at a loss for words for the pain and suffering that I was going through.

We walked back to the cubicle, and as we got there, the hospital porter was there to take my auntie to ward 5, so, as like before with both my mam and dad, I followed through the corridors that I knew only too well. We arrived at ward 5, and as we made our way through towards reception, I saw the familiar faces and could smell the same smells as if I had not been away from there.

My auntie was taken into a room which had other patients in it, and I saw a familiar face lying in the bed next to my auntie. She was Mrs Catlin, and she only lived two doors away from my aunt. She recognised my auntie as soon as we entered. She asked me, 'What's wrong with Meredith?'

'We aren't sure yet. She's not herself, so we called for the doctor, who then called for an ambulance to bring her to be looked at. They brought her to this ward to be cared for and find out what's wrong with her.'

The staff got my auntie Meredith settled into her bed. Jane and I were allowed to stay for a while before being asked to leave by the staff.

As we left my auntie to settle down, I saw the face of a female nurse who knew me from my time in the ward with my mother and father, and she was the same one I went to school with. She came over to me and asked what I was doing back in here.

'I'm here with my auntie. She is all that I have left of my family, so will you take good care of her for me?'

'Yes, we will. You get home and look after yourself. You look worn out.'

I replied, 'I can't believe the bad luck that I keep suffering. I was only in hospital myself two weeks ago. I was in an accident on my bike and had a head-on crash with a car.'

'Oh my God, you have had bad things happen, Daniel, what with your mam and dad and now your auntie. I don't know what to say.'

'Just take care of my auntie for me; she is all that is left of my family. If you need me, here is my phone number.'

She wrote my number in the book and asked, 'Is there anything else I can do before you go?'

'Yes, will you phone my brother Spencer to inform him that our auntie has been taken to hospital and has been admitted to this ward?'

'Yes, leave that to me. I'll do that for you.'

'Thank you, Anna,' I replied, giving her his number. I then made my way out of ward 5 once more.

I walked to Jane's car, as she'd said she would drop me off at my flat to save me getting a taxi home. I told Jane on the way home that I hoped nothing happened to Auntie Meredith. 'She will be fine. She's in good hands there.'

'I know, but that's the same ward where my mam passed away in while in my arms, and it's the same ward that I was in with my dad when he had his stroke. I'm going to lose another member of my family in some way or another in the same ward 5. I can't cope with any more bad things. Am I going to have to watch my auntie Meredith pass away in the same hospital?'

Jane tried to reassure me by saying, 'Your auntie Meredith will be fine. She's a tough old woman. She'll be home in no time.'

'I hope you're right,' I said as she dropped me off at my flat.

I made my way into my flat and sat down. I was worn out, traumatised, distraught, and an emotional wreck of a man yet again. I picked my phone up and called Gabrielle to inform her once more of a loved one in hospital and in the same ward 5 that her granddad and nana were in.

She was speechless as I told her. She could not believe what I was telling her. She broke down in tears and told me that she wanted to come down to be with me.

'I'll be, OK, Gabrielle. Come down tomorrow and we will go to the hospital and see Auntie Meredith together at visiting times.' I arranged for her to visit, and afterwards I sat in my chair, reflecting on what had happened to me again and the thought of having to go through everything all over again with my auntie as before with my mam and dad.

I couldn't settle, so I got in my car, which was still very difficult to drive since my bike accident, and I managed to drive down to the cemetery to go to my parents' graveside. I broke down in tears in front of the headstone, telling my mam and dad that Auntie Meredith had been taken to hospital and I was not coping well and suffering alone, with no help or support from anyone other than

Gabrielle, who was my rock, my tower of strength, the only person in my life whom I was keeping it together for. I said that I wasn't sure how much more I could take.

I sat in tears as darkness fell, and then I picked myself up from the ground, telling my mam and dad how much I was missing them and how lost I had become without them in my life. I lit two candles and then made my way to my car and drove home, falling into bed as soon as I got there. I was a physical and emotional wreck of a person.

I woke up during the night screaming in fear and covered in sweat, as with my past traumas. I was once again in a flood of tears, panicking and traumatised. I sat in the corner of my bedroom on the cold floor, a complete broken and shaking wreck. I had just had a nightmare of all the bad things that I had suffered with. It was so vivid and totally terrifying that I threw my guts up and was saturated and soaked in sweat with fear of it.

This experience was like the flip pages of my accident standing still on pause like a film on a disc. The nightmare was like reliving every catastrophic trauma again and again, second by second, minute by minute. I just wanted it to end. After an hour or so, I pulled myself together and ran a bath for myself. I had a long soak in the bath and sat awake the rest of the night until the safety of daylight, in which I felt safe and secure. I waited till 8 a.m. and phoned my doctors up for an emergency appointment with Dr Janice at 10 a.m.

Making my way to the surgery, I drove round to Auntie Meredith's bungalow to open the curtains and check that everything was OK. I informed a few of her neighbours that Auntie Meredith was in hospital and asked if they could please keep an eye out on her bungalow for me. They agreed and said to tell her that they sent their love. I told them that I would pass their regards to her when I visited her in the afternoon.

Leaving the bungalow to drive to the surgery, I stopped at my mam and dad's home, which had a for sale sign on it. I walked in and wander around the empty shell of what used to be my family home that was filled with happy times. Now it just felt like a cold, shallow, empty shell, with no reminders showing or bearing any signs that my mother gave birth to me in her bedroom with the midwife in 1968 or that I had lived there for so long with my parents. I felt very empty and lost. I left, vowing never to return to it.

Now in the surgery, my name was called out, and I slowly got to my feet and made my way to Dr Janice's room. She probably thought that I was there because of the accident that I had been involved in. She asked me, 'How are you coping? Are you still in pain?'

'Yes, my body is killing me, but that's not why I have come to see you.'

I broke down in tears. 'I'm here because I have been in hospital again yesterday, for another reason this time. It's my auntie Meredith. She was rushed there yesterday and has been admitted into the same ward 5 that my mam and dad were in, and I am not coping with it all. I cannot take any more.'

She told me that she didn't know what to say. Again, she was also my auntie Meredith's doctor and knew her very well, as she had my mam and dad. We talked for about an hour or so, and I told her about the nightmares I had been having, as well as all the other things that had happened to me, and she gave me a course of mild antidepressant to try to relax me and help me cope with the traumatic and difficult times ahead of me. A further appointment was made for me, and I left to pick up my daughter.

Now with Gabrielle with me, we went to my flat, where we chatted and comforted each other, trying to make sense of everything that had fallen upon our family. Unable to make sense of it all, we both ended up in tears, stressed and worn out, tense and anxious as we made our way to hospital ward 5 to visit Auntie Meredith.

As we once again arrive to the car park and made out way to the hospital entrance, I turned to Gabrielle and said, 'I hope my brother Spencer isn't here. I don't want to bump into him, as I don't think I will be able to stop myself from dragging him outside and putting him in hospital over all his accusations of fraud over my father's money and pestering Auntie Meredith with it all.'

'If he's here, Dad, we'll go and come back another time.'

'No, why should I go anywhere? I won't kick off with him; I am better than that, Gabrielle. Your nana and granddad brought me up better than that, and I would disappoint them if I did do anything. After all, he is not worth it. He can live the rest of his selfish, pathetic life with his own guilt of knowing he never lifted a finger to help me care for Mam and Dad or Auntie Meredith. He knows he could have done far more to look after them and nana and Granddad, and Auntie Meredith also knew he could, so if he is here, he can leave when we get there.'

We headed to the elevators and got off at the first floor, entering ward 5. At this stage, I was feeling anxiety levels race through the roof as well as fear and apprehension. The flashing images of my mother passing away in my arms wouldn't leave my mind, and shivers ran down my spine. I held a tight grip on Gabrielle's hand for comfort as we made our way past reception and into the side ward where my auntie was. Straight away I saw my brother Spencer with his wife.

My heart rate soared with anger, but I composed myself and said to my daughter, 'Let's go to the cafe and get a drink. He might have gone when we return.'

Whilst we sat having coffee, I opened my wallet to look at the appointment card I was given when I was in hospital in A&E only two weeks ago. The appointment was to return to A&E to have my stitches removed from my right thigh, in which I had over twenty-five stitches from the bike accident. Looking at Gabrielle, I told her that I had to go to A&E the next day at tomorrow at 1 p.m. to have my stitches removed.

'I bet you're not looking forward to that,' she replied.

'No, I'm not, but as I am here now and to pass some time while my brother is with Auntie Meredith, I am going to go now and have them removed.'

'Is that a good thing to do, Dad? Your head's in bits now. I don't think you should do that.'

'Well, I am already stressed out and anxious, tense, and upset. I may as well face the fears of returning to A&E and save doing it tomorrow. At least I have you here now to support me.'

'OK, if you are sure you want to do this, then let's go.'

We made our way to the A&E. At reception, I told them I was actually here visiting my auntie on ward 5. I explained my difficulties about being in hospital again so soon after my accident and that I had an appointment for the next day but wanted the stitches removed now, while I had my daughter here for comfort and support.

'Take a seat Mr Osborne and we'll get you looked at.'

We sat down in the reception area. Gabrielle could tell I was on edge. She could see the fear in my eyes as I became ever more distressed at being back in A&E, back to where all the faces of staff were so recognisable.

I was becoming more and more anxious to get the stitches out so I could leave as soon as possible and get away from A&E to never return again.

'Mr Osborne,' I heard in the distance.

I looked around to see a nurse calling me, so I headed towards her. My heart was beating faster and faster, and my arms and legs felt heavy and weak as I walked towards the cubicle area for patients.

I looked over to the left side and saw the cubicle in which I was fighting for my life only weeks earlier. I instantly started to have flashbacks and images, sights and smells of everything that I had suffered on that dreadful, frightening, life-threatening, traumatising day of events. The nurse showed me into a different cubicle away from the other side where I was. She recognised my face from that fateful day and saw that I was in distress and uncomfortable with the surroundings of A&E. She got me a glass of water and sat with me to help calm me down and slow my breathing down, which after a while helped me slightly. I composed myself and relaxed a bit.

I was now asked by the nurse, 'Are you ready to have your stitches taken out now, Mr Osborne?'

'Yes, let's get this over with as quickly as possible,' I replied.

I lay down on my front on a bed, and she began to remove the stitches from my thigh. Whilst she was removing them, the ruminating, flashing images, all the bad reminders of my accident, the sights and the sounds, the images of looking inside my open wound, the images of all the blood I was soaked and lying in for six hours, and the noise from the MRI scan machine were ringing through my ears. I saw myself hitting the car and heard my body smashing with the impact. I saw all the flashing blue lights from the ambulance. I began to hear the sirens and became overwhelmed with how real and how vivid it was. I screamed out with fear and panic as stitches were being removed. It was as if the accident had only just happened.

The nurse removed the final few stitches, and she told me that the wound was healing nicely. She helped me stand up to my feet. I felt overcome and dizzy, so she helped me sit in a chair.

'Would you go get my daughter, please? I need to get out of here. I feel sick, as if I'm going to pass out.'

Gabrielle was brought in, and we left the A&E to make our way back to ward 5 to see if my brother Spencer had left. Thankfully, he had.

Gabrielle and I sat down at Auntie Meredith's side. Mrs Catlin and her husband, who lived two doors from my aunt Meredith, said hello to me. Gabrielle and I started chatting with Auntie Meredith. *She seems and looks OK*, I thought.

We stayed for the duration of visiting times, and she told us that my brother and his wife had been to visit. I just said, 'Oh, right. At least he has been to see you.' I told her that her bungalow was fine and that I was going every day to check it and put lights on, adding that the neighbours were also keeping a close eye on it. I told her not to worry over it, to relax and get herself better so she could return home.

It comforted her knowing the bungalow was safe. She said, 'Thank you, Daniel. I don't know what I would do without you.'

I told her that I would always look after her as I had with Mam and Dad. 'I promised my dad that I would continue to look after you for him and to make sure you are OK.'

Visiting times ended, and we said goodbye to Auntie Meredith, telling her we would see her tomorrow.

I asked on the way out if the doctors had any idea what was up with my auntie. They said it was too early to tell but that maybe it was some sort of flu or cold. They said they would know more as time went on and that they would keep me informed as to my auntie' condition.

'Thank you, Doctor. If there is any change, you have my contact details to phone me.'

We made haste to get out of the hospital as quickly as possible, as my head was done in once more from being there. We went to my auntie Meredith's bungalow on the way home and looked in her address phone book to see whom I needed to contact to inform them she was in hospital, as she also had relatives who lived in Scotland and were from her late husband's side.

I rang and informed various people whom I had met or spoken with about my auntie Meredith's condition, and they arranged to travel from Scotland to see her. I think it was my late uncle's brother who came from Scotland to see my auntie Meredith. He'd stayed in my aunt's bungalow while he visited, and I remembered him staying for a few days, which turned out to be nice for my auntie, as she was always close to and kept in contact with that side of her family.

Things pretty much stayed the same for about three weeks or more. I continued to go to visit every day, twice a day, as hard as it was for me, as I genuinely had built up a fear of this hospital. I was on red alert every time I pulled into the grounds of it. I was always expecting something bad to happen to me because each time I visited my auntie Meredith, she was showing no real signs of getting better or returning home.

Now my brain was telling me to expect and prepare itself for that next bad thing to happen to me and to rip my life apart once again, and it was looking as if it was going to be the same ward 5 where my mother passed away in my arms! But these were only thoughts, which I tried to put to the back of my mind and forget about them. I tried not to let these thoughts enter my mind, but with everything that had happened to me in

this hospital in such a short time of each other, all within twelve months of each other. Was it any wonder my mind was acting like this and thinking this way? I had lost so much and suffered so much in such a short period of time. This was why I had become somewhat switched on with that red alert button of danger and bad things happening to me. I felt that each day I was awaiting further distressing bad news!

Three weeks had now passed with my auntie in hospital. The date was 14 September 2008, which meant that in five days' time, it would have been my dad's eighty-sixth birthday and was also only eight days away from 22September 2008, a year ago to the day that my father had a stroke in my arms and was taken to the hospital ward that my auntie Meredith was now still in and I was visiting for the second time that day. The doctors were still unsure what was wrong and said it was flulike. I sat chatting with her for the night. As we chatted, Jane showed up to visit, which pleased my auntie.

Jane asked about my auntie. She also asked how I was and if I was coping OK, and I told her that I was managing the best I could under the circumstances.

I then heard a voice behind me, and my body cringed at the sound of it. It was my brother Spencer. He'd showed up to visit. I kissed my auntie good night and told her I would be back for visiting times tomorrow afternoon.

I then said goodbye to Jane and left, walking past my brother, wanting to drag him outside and give him a good beating. I didn't make a scene in front of everybody, and I left the hospital to return the next day for visiting times.

I was at home now, trying to relax as best I could. I took my tablets which my doctor prescribed, the antidepressants and the tablets for the pain my body was still going through since my accident. I woke up again during the night, screaming and soaked in sweat. Another nightmare had woken me up—a terrifying one about my time alone with my mother when she passed away in my arms. I stayed awake for the rest of the night, unable to fall back to sleep. I watched a bit of TV. The time was now 10 a.m.

On 15 September 2008, I drove down to my Auntie Meredith's bungalow to open curtains up and switch lights off. I then heard my phone ring in my pocket. I instantly sensed something *bad* straight away, before I had even looked at it or answered it, and the hairs on my neck stood on end. A cold shiver ran through my spine once more. I looked at the phone as I retrieved it from my jacket pocket. I recognised the number straight away. It was the reception number of ward 5. I thought, *Not again. Please don't be bad news like I have had before in the past.*

The female voice asked, 'Is this Mr Osborne?'

I answered yes with a lump stuck in my throat.

'I'm phoning regarding your aunt Meredith. Are you her nephew and next of kin?' I said I was, and she said, 'Your auntie has taken a turn for the worse. I think it would be a good idea for you to make your way to the hospital to be with her.'

'I'm on my way. I'll be there in ten minutes.' I asked if they would inform my brother Spencer as to Auntie Meredith's condition.

'I will ring now,' she told me.

My head was in bits. I couldn't believe it. Not again. Not my auntie. Don't take her away from me as well. I would have no family left, no one other than Gabrielle. It would only be her and me left. We would have no one else left to call family to love and cherish.

I arrived at hospital and made my way to ward 5, where I'd lost my mother a year ago, all the time terrified that I may be going back to the same ward to lose another loved one in my arms.

I was frightened, alone, in shock and overcome with emotion, with flashing reminders of losing my mother in my arms. I entered ward 5 once more. I dashed down to my auntie Meredith's bedside, and the doctor stopped me on the way, informing me that she had taken a turn for the worse. Hearing those words, I knew straight away what he was trying to prepare me for.

I went to my auntie Meredith's side. I saw Mrs Catlin still in her bed and her husband still sat at her side next to my auntie. I saw in their eyes that they knew what I was about to suffer and go through.

The doctor came in with me and closed the curtains around me, leaving me to be alone with my auntie Meredith. I held her hands and asked her what was up. I was trying to be strong. 'Is everything OK, Auntie?'

I felt her taking a tighter grip of my hands, and she told me that she loved Gabrielle and me and would always watch over us both.

I said, 'You're not going anywhere, Auntie Meredith. I have lost my mam and dad. I can't lose you as well. What will I do then? Who will care for Gabrielle and me and love us? I will have nothing left of my family.'

As I told her how much I loved her and how much Gabrielle would miss her, she then looked into my eyes, just as my beautiful mother had a year ago in the same ward. I held her in my arms, shouting for her not to leave me alone. 'Please don't leave me, Auntie Meredith. Please don't go.' Tears were streaming down my face, and she glanced up at me, a smile on her loving face. Then she passed away peacefully in my arms in the exact same way that my mother had, just she and I together, no one else—no other family for support and no one to comfort me with my pain. There would be no tender loving words of comfort for me to hear.

I was holding my auntie Meredith in my arms, sobbing as I had with my mam, uncontrollable tears pouring from my eyes and in shock, totally traumatised. I called for help, and the doctors and nurses who were looking after my auntie came to my aid. Some faces seemed recognisable from when I had lost my mother. They took me to a quiet room. As I passed Mr and Mrs Catlin, they told me how sorry they were for my loss.

Now traumatised and alone in a room, I broke down, trying to make sense of why bad things kept happening to me. Had God abandoned me? Was I such an awful person to have so much pain and suffering to be inflicted on me. I questioned any beliefs I had in the man above. Did he want me to suffer all of my life? Would it ever stop?

The doctor came in after a while and told me he was sorry for my loss and that they needed to do what needed to be done and that there was no need for me to stay other than if I wanted to collect my auntie Meredith's belongings once they had taken her from the ward. I said I'd stay so I could collect her belongings to take them with me.

I thought, *I hope I can get them out before my brother turns up, if he does turn up.*

A short time after that, I was allowed to gather my auntie Meredith's belongings. The doctor asked me to sign the necessary documents. After doing so, I left the hospital before my brother turned up. I was glad, as I would have now swung for him at this point.

I left the hospital thinking that I had nothing else to lose or be taken away from me. I never wanted to return here, at least not for a very long time. To this day, I'm still unsure whether my so-called brother ever showed up there.

I made my way home, calling at the cemetery on the way to go to my parents' headstone. I broke down in front of it and told my mam and dad that I was sorry. I'd done everything that I could, but my aunt had just passed away in my arms in hospital. I have lost all of you and have just me and Gabrielle. Keep a watchful eye over us both.

I left the graveside and returned to my auntie's bungalow. I called Gabrielle and informed her that we had lost Auntie Meredith. She was heartbroken, lost for words and in tears, and once again found herself in the arms of her mother to be comforted. I told her I was OK and would ring her later. I then phoned everyone in my auntie's address book and informed them that my auntie Meredith had just passed away.

After leaving my auntie's bungalow, I drove to Dr Janice's office and told her that I had lost another family member in hospital and in the same ward as I had lost my mother. She could not believe her ears and was speechless as she gave me a sedative to relax me. I went home to my flat traumatised for the fourth time in twelve months.

I struggled to relax, finding myself wandering aimlessly from room to room, trying to make sense of all that I had lost and loved for all of my life. This is a brief recollection of all that I thought about. My mother had a fall and as a result ended up needing to be cared for and was admitted to a nursing home where she was a resident for five years, suffering with dementia, and I became a carer for my elderly father, whom I'd looked after and taken to the nursing home every day twice a day whilst also caring for my auntie.

My mother was taken into hospital and passed away in my arms in ward 5. My father had a stroke in my arms in the home I was born in and was also taken to hospital, to ward 5, He was then transferred to another hospital, where he passed away in my arms, only four months apart from each other. I was then left alone and looking after my remaining family members. I had a bike accident that could have killed me, and I was once again back in hospital fighting for my own life. Miraculously, I survived and went home. Then two weeks later, my auntie Meredith was taken to the same hospital and passed away in my arms in the same ward 5 as my mother.

How could things possibly get any worse for me? Nothing else bad could happen to me. I had nothing else to lose.

Now that you have read my book, I want to explain how I was diagnosed with PTSD and the treatment that I have had to help me have a better understanding of it.

After all the traumas that I encountered in my life, and all in such a short period, my life started to gain some normality once I lost all of my family between August 3rd and September 8 and survived my accident. Christmas 2009 was approaching, and the sale of my parents' home was finished, thanks to the quickness of my so-called brother's intervention, wanting his inheritance. I was now heading for a breakdown—the thought of Christmas with no mother, father, and auntie for the first time in my life was looming ever so closer.

It was now the middle of November, and I couldn't stand the thought of Christmas alone. My father had passed away over the Christmas season. I decide to surprise Gabrielle, and I booked a last-minute winter holiday to Fuerteventura, Canary Islands, to escape being around the prospect of spending the festive period alone. If I would have stayed, I don't think I would have been here today writing this book, as I was close to questioning the foundations of my own existence. I wanted to be with my parents and auntie, as I felt lost without them.

I sprang the surprise on my daughter when having her stay one weekend, and while we were down at the cemetery paying our respects, I put the tickets in front of her and told her we were going away for Christmas. She said, 'Dad, are we really?'

'Yes, we are going to spend Christmas away.' The thought of spending it here was torturing me.

She was so overjoyed. The smile on her face was fantastic. We were to fly on 24 December 2008 and stay for two weeks. This worked out well so that we would be away for the periods of the date of losing my father and the date of his burial.

We arrived at Fuerteventura for Christmas Day and went for a meal. We relaxed away from the strains and pressures that we had both suffered.

We instantly fell in love with Fuerteventura. It is truly a beautiful island, with crystal clear waters surrounded with white sand. I booked many different excursions for us to take our minds away from the heartache we had left behind.

We took a quad bike tour of the island and went to a magnificent safari park. We also went on a cruise for the day on a yacht, a day trip to Lanzarote, and loads of other trips out, including a night out to a drag show, which was excellent. I had never seen my Gabrielle enjoy herself so much. It was the highlight of the holiday for her.

In between doing all the excursions, my daughter asked me to stop smoking, which most people know is hard to do. Even my doctor said that with everything that I had gone through, it was not a good idea for me to try to stop. But I'd promised my daughter that I would stop. I threw my cigarettes in the bin in the hotel room and decided to go for a run along the white sands.

I only lasted a day or two and then bought a packet of cigarettes. I went to have one and saw the look of disappointment written all over my daughter's face. I had broken a promise and failed her, so I then crushed them up and put them in the bin and tried again. The day I stopped smoking forever was on the 29 December 2008, a year to the day that my father passed away in my arms. This time of stopping had a purpose, a meaning of change. I told my daughter how much I loved her, and from this day onwards, I will never smoke again. She saw the look of determination on my face.

I put my training shoes on and went for an eight-mile run in the beautiful weather. I stopped for a while and sat on a rock to catch my breath. I sit there for a while knowing the day it was and that a year has passed since my father passed away. I shed all my tears for not just my dad but my mam and auntie Meredith as well.

After an hour or so of looking out to the sea and admiring the place that surrounded me, I jogged back to the hotel and went to the gym, sauna, and Jacuzzi. I loved it so much that I felt that this island was the place where I belonged. Gabrielle continued to enjoy the holiday, and as each day passed, I would go for my run and use the gym daily without even thinking about wanting a cigarette.

We passed into the new year, and I promised my daughter I would continue not to smoke when we returned home. 'We will see, Dad,' she said.

'To be honest, I stopped on the anniversary of losing your granddad. That day was the turning point for me,' I said.

When we arrived home, I took Gabrielle to the cemetery with me. We paid our respects after comforting each other while standing at my parents' headstone, which, to my shock, had no wreaths on it. I told Gabrielle how disgusted I was over the lack of respect from Spencer. She said, 'I thought he would have at least made the effort for them for Christmas, Dad.'

'You would have thought so, Gabrielle. Just goes to show you, doesn't it?'

We left the cemetery, and I then took her home to her mother's.

After I dropped Gabrielle off, I made my way home and headed straight to a gym in my local town. I'd joined up front as an incentive for me to keep off the cigarettes and get fit.

At this present day in time, I have never had another cigarette and have been going to the gym for over eight years, something that I am very proud of doing. It was done with sheer determination and with the help of no smoking aids. I am very proud of this positive accomplishment.

When I got home, I tried to return into employment as an asbestos operative with my close friends whom I had worked with and known for many years and have always regarded as family. They were like the brothers I never had. We worked on various jobs during the year of 2009, but while were away, I started having some terrifying flashbacks of my bike accident while in the working area with my full face mask on, which you must wear when working with asbestos. The mask that one wears when working with asbestos has a full clear visor that is only an inch or so away from touching your face.

The flashbacks that I had were flashing images of my face smashing into the windscreen of the car, and the visor of the mask made me feel distraught and reminded me of the accident. I began to hyperventilate and panic. I felt as if I had to remove the mask to try get some air, but you can't just remove it in a working area. You have to come from the work area wearing your mask and go through a decontamination unit.

I ran out of the work area in fear, terrified, screaming, 'Get me out of here! Get this mask off me!' I ran for the decontamination unit and showered properly before removing the mask that was reminding me of smashing into the windscreen of the car.

I got dressed and left the place of work to return to my hotel, where I sat for the rest of the day, asking myself, *Am I losing my mind? Am I cracking up? Is this normal? What is wrong with me?*

My friends finished their shift and returned to the hotel, making their way to my room to see if I was OK. I assured them that I was and said I didn't wish to talk about it.

I tried to return to work and not think too much about it, hoping that it wouldn't happen again, but how wrong I was! I had further panic attacks and flashbacks, images of impacting the car on the day of my accident, which wouldn't leave me alone. I feared for my health and pulling my mask off in a working area, thereby exposing myself to asbestos and putting my life at risk. I decided to return from working away and wearing a mask that kept reminding me of my accident.

I made an appointment to see Dr Janice and explained to her the ruminating recurring flashbacks that I kept having. She said that they were symptoms of PTSD. It's commonly associated with people who have suffered a traumatic event in their life. PTSD is a combination of reactions following a traumatic event. 'Unfortunately for you, Daniel,' she said, 'you have not just suffered one traumatic event; you have suffered four different traumas all on your own, with little help from your siblings, and you have only had the love and support of your daughter. It's no wonder you are feeling the way you have been. I want you to see a counsellor to discuss your problems, so I will arrange for them to start in the surgery and will contact you in the coming weeks to let you know when I have this arranged.'

'OK, Doctor. Thank you so much for listening to me. Is there anything else I need to know?'

'Yes. The flashbacks you are having are the reminders of past traumas and bad events that you have suffered. This is only the beginning. There is a lot worse lying ahead of you. But I will get the counselling sessions arranged as soon as I can.'

My counselling started at the surgery with a psychologist named Dr Mason. At our first meeting, I told him about the four traumas that I had suffered in the last sixteen months. He was struck for words. 'You've had it rough. I cannot believe you have gone through so much,' he said.

He continued to ask about the past. I only told him what I felt comfortable with. I didn't go into detail. After all, he was a stranger to me. However, I would find myself staying awake most nights, not wanting to go to sleep or to close my eyes in case of a nightmare. This is how my life would continue for the next several years, even to the present day.

My sessions continued with my counsellor for about eight weeks. Then he moved to another area, so it was impossible for me to continue to see him for therapy.

Each day brought its own challenge for me, constantly battling to keep my mind sane and not lose the plot altogether. But as the constant battles continued, I still felt fearful. The fear of going out and seeing my friends was becoming harder for me. How could they possibly understand what I was going through? How would they feel if they had lost all of their family in their arms in less than twelve months and nearly lost their own life in an accident? But they knew me better than any of my own brothers and sisters, and I respected each of them, as they had been there for me when I lost my parents and auntie. I had worked with most of them for many years. I would do anything for any of them.

But in the later months of 2009, a lot of them started to treat me differently. They would stop keeping in touch or calling up to see me. One of them I had confided in about something very personal of a delicate nature. He rang the other mates of mine whom I was meeting for a drink and broke my trust. He told one of my other mates about what I had talked to him in confidence, and as I walked into the pub where I was meeting them in, I walked to the bar, got a drink, and sat down with the same crowd of friends, about twelve or more. I was completely disgusted that they were all having a laugh at my expense about what I told my friend earlier. So thanks, lads. Just goes to show what you really thought about our friendship, only to stab me in the back and kick me when I was already down with everything that I had suffered and lost.

I left the pub with all my close mates still taking the piss out of me. I rang the mate I had confided in and told him that I would never trust him again, that he had betrayed me over such a personal matter. 'How could you do that to me?' I asked.

He said that he should have known better and that he should not have told my other friend. I said, 'Well, thanks to you, I have been made a laughingstock in front of friends. Thanks a bunch, mate.'

Things were difficult in my life without my best friends treating me like shit and breaking my trust. But in the coming weeks, things were patched up and we remained friends, but not for long.

My personal life was getting no better in regards to the nightmares, waking up screaming with fear, bed-wetting,, and having flashbacks and reminders of past traumas. The slightest thing would remind me of different traumas, and life became a struggle to get through each day.

All of the days that are important to most families, like Mother's Day, Father's Day, and so on, were extremely difficult to cope with, and nearly every day, without fail, I'd go to the cemetery to be close to my parents.

I tried once again to face one of my fears and return to work wearing my asbestos mask, but this did not last long. I found myself incapable of doing the job that I had once loved doing due to the panic attacks. Wearing the mask was too much of a reminder of my face smashing into the windscreen of the car. Each time that I donned my mask, I would have a flashback of my accident and would see the driver's face as if it were in front of me as I smashed into her car.

It was nearing the end of November 2009 and approaching the time of year that I dreaded the most, wishing and longing to return to Fuerteventura. I wanted to get away from it all once more, but I was unable to go. I had to face up to another Christmas alone since losing my family. But that time of year came, and I dreaded the thought of it so much.

Gabrielle came to stay for a few days for Christmas, which we both struggled to cope with. We made the best of what we had and went to the cemetery together. We placed some wreaths there for my mam and dad, and surprise, surprise, there was nothing from any other family member placed upon my parents' graveside. I turned to Gabrielle and said, 'Well, I wasn't really expecting there to be anything when no one other than you and I have left anything for them.'

'I know, Dad. It's a shame. You would have thought that at least this time of year someone would have bothered to come other than us. It was only you and I when they were alive.'

Gabrielle returned home to be with her mother and sisters. It was nice to have her down to support me. She truly is the best daughter in the world.

I returned to the cemetery on 29 December 2009. It had been two years since my dad had passed away. I placed another wreath and stayed for a few hours to be as close as I could be to both my mam and dad. I went through all the emotions and broke down in bits.

I made my way home and reflected on times of late. I drank a bottle of vodka to help cope with how I felt. I passed out in my chair in the front room. However, it did not stop the nightmares I was hoping not to have.

The next day, I just sat in my flat alone, with only my thoughts for comfort. Time drifted by, and I found myself standing in my bedroom. It had become night-time once more, and the thoughts of even going to bed and closing my eyes were too overwhelming. I sat awake most of the night, but I did manage to get some sleep.

Now it was New Year's Eve 2009, and the friend who'd betrayed me asked I wanted to go to his brother's for a drink to celebrate. He was one of my good friends and a work colleague. I didn't really want to be around people, but he said, 'Get yourself down. It will do you good.'

I went down at about 7 p.m., taking a bottle of vodka as a gift. There were other friends there as well, and I suppose the company did me some good instead of being on my own. But towards midnight, I wished that I had never gone, as my so-called friends decided once more to have their say and tell me what they thought. One of them said, 'Daniel, you don't smoke anymore. You are overweight and antisocial because you don't smoke.'

I said, 'How on earth am I antisocial? If I were, I wouldn't be here talking and drinking with you all.'

'Yeah, but you're not the same person anymore.'

I had heard this before. Do these words sound familiar to you? You tell yourself or the person saying it to you, 'What do you expect? You have no idea what you're saying—unless you suffer with PTSD as I do. Do you have no understanding of what trauma is like and, in my case, four traumas in twelve months? Keep your words to yourself. If you have nothing good to say to me, then don't say anything at all.'

Those were the types of words offered to me as a means of support, and hearing these words from friends I had known for years made me sick to the stomach. I left the party and went home full of anger at the insensitivity.

I started the new year making a promise to myself not to keep allowing friends to treat me the way they had in the past. The days and weeks began to roll by with no signs of showing any improvement with my flashbacks and daily ruminating of my bike accident, hospitals, and ambulances.

I was invited out around March 2010 and reluctantly went. We all ended up back at my flat, where we socialised until the early hours. I was later to find out from a mate who was here that night and was sober at the time that during the course of the night, my so-called best friends were standing in my kitchen happily telling my sober friend that now these are the exact words used by the way whilst using my hospitality and comforts of my home they told my sober mate. 'Yeah, fuck him in there,' meaning me. I sat in my front living room while they were in my kitchen slagging me. 'After tonight, we are through. I don't want fuck all to do with him.'

These friends had the balls to stay that about me in my own home. Fucking shame they couldn't say it in front of me.

Apparently, because I had lost my parents, had a major accident, and had stopped smoking for over a year, I was no longer the same person and was not worthy of being a friend any longer.

Well, I'd say it's their loss, not mine. What a pathetic use to throw a friendship of sixteen years or more away because I had stopped smoking and didn't stand outside pubs in the rain having a cigarette with them. I had enough shit to cope with in my life without the hassle of having people in my home saying things like that about me. One day when they lose a loved one or three and nearly lose their own lives, they might look back and remember what they said to me and how wrong it was, but I very much doubt it.

It was April 2010, and I was suffering with a ruptured hernia from the previous year, a result of lifting too much weight at the gym. I decided to do some volunteer work for a local charity that helps families with poorly children with underlying health issues. I approached the manager and asked if I could do some painting and decorating for them. NOW is a charity for which my late auntie Meredith used to do a lot of charity work for. The manager at the time showed me a long corridor where they had a children's sensory room, which was filled with lots of different reflective lights. The room had a fibre optic carpet, water bubble lamps filled with toy fish, projectors that shined lights onto walls, as well as many other ways to keep the children occupied. I called it a chill out room for kids; it was a truly special room. He said that I could paint the corridor to brighten it up, so I made a design for the corridor and transformed it from a dull peach-coloured corridor into a bright multicoloured one that looked better and was more appropriate for the nature of the charity. Below are a couple of photos to show how it looks now.

My late auntie Meredith did so much for different charities as well as for this one. When her bungalow was sold, she left most of the proceeds to charity. They were unaware of what I was doing. I'd kept it a secret. They both came into the room with a photographer from the local evening gazette, as they were covering the story of my auntie's good gesture to this local charity. The first words were, 'Hello, what are you doing back here?'

I said, 'I have something for you to see. Look what I have installed in the sensory room for the kids to look at when they are in here.' I got them to remove the cover and see the picture. I switched it on and showed them.

They were overjoyed with it. 'Daniel, that's beautiful. That thank you so much.'

I told both of the managers to take a closer look at the piece of paper that was on the picture. They stepped closer and saw that I had placed a cheque there for £32,000. They couldn't believe their eyes and were blown away with emotion at the gesture from my auntie Meredith. It was a proud moment in my life that fulfilled a promise I'd made to my late auntie Meredith.

Below are images of the freshly painted children's corridor that I painted to brighten the place up a little for the families that use this charity.

Both managers and the rest of the staff were over the moon with how it now looked. They were both lost for words at all that I had done for them. The children in their care made me a hand-painted card with the words 'Thank you for all that you have done for us.' It was one of the nicest gestures of thanks I had ever received. I remember opening the letter when it arrived by post. There were many pages of drawings and pictures. I was overcome, to say the least.

I tried once more to return to work in the month of June, but not for asbestos, just labouring for some pipe lagging company on a power station down at the other end of the country. It only lasted for a week and ended up a disaster. I should have known better.

Now back home, I went to see my doctor, as I was not coping at all with all the daily flashbacks and nightmares. She saw how bad things were with me, and once more she helped me see a counsellor for therapy. This time it was with a place called Talk Time, based in a local town. It was with a great person called Damian, whom I felt comfortable with straight away. I also told my doctor that I was having many problems with pain from my groin area. She examined me and informed me that I was going to need surgery for an inguinal ruptured hernia. I told her that I was not going to go anywhere near that hospital again. I had gone through too much even to think about returning there, no matter what the circumstances.

She told me that I must have the surgery. It could cause serious damage if left untreated. There had to be another way. I said, 'Anywhere other than there!'

'There is one place where I can get you looked at. It's called the Life Centre Clinic.'

I instantly felt a sigh of relief come over me. So she arranged for me to have an appointment for a check-up.

'Thank you, Doctor. How long will it take to hear from them?'

She told me that it would be about six to eight weeks. She also gave me my prescription for an antidepressant and the sleeping tablets that she had put me on over a year ago after my accident. Hopefully, I could get at least one or two nights of good sleep during the week.

I had my surgery on 18 October 2010, six days before my birthday. I was obviously apprehensive about going into hospital again, but I was in and out in five hours and made a full recovery. I continued to go to the gym every day.

I continued to see my therapist, Damian. Over the course of time, I opened up to him more and more. Each time that I went to see him he pushed me to discuss each of the traumas that I had suffered. I found doing this extremely difficult. I would break down each time, overcome with anxiety.

Damian was very understanding and good at what he was doing. He needed to know my fears, the way I was thinking, and how I was reacting to and coping with the traumas I had suffered. He started to use different techniques on me, things like mindfulness of the breath and body as well as sounds, thoughts, and emotions. When I talked with him about my traumas, I would become anxious. We practiced some breathing and body techniques to help me reduce my levels of anxiety and to help me bring myself back into the present time, away from the past traumas of what would be upsetting and disturbing to me.

We made good use of these techniques with great effects that helped me to focus on where I was and things I could see or touch, like the feel of the arms on the chair I was sitting in. He would help me focus on different sights and sounds in my environment to bring me back to the present and not the past. He also gave me a CD with different techniques as to how to use them at home for when things got difficult.

As the sessions with Damian seemed to be going well, I allowed myself to trust him. I openly discussed my problematic traumas that I was suffering from, and he wanted me to talk in detail to him about my bike accident. I told him the story from the moment that I'd left my flat to where I'd travelled, telling him everything, missing no details.

After six or maybe seven sessions with Damian, I was referred to another professional psychologist, an expert in the field of treatment of PTSD, a gentleman whom Damian and my own Dr Janice spoke very highly of.

I thanked Damian for everything that he had done for me, and he wished me well for the future. Now waiting for my first session with another therapist, I became anxious once more about having to explain my traumas all over again to another psychologist and to have to allow this person to gain my trust, as I did with Damian.

My first session with Dr Williamson was uncomfortable. His approach was a bit strange. He would sit close in a chair, all the time staring into my face. But I got the first session done, and it lasted for over two hours. I could tell instantly from this first encounter with Dr Williamson that I thought he would be able to help me and make me have a better understanding of recognising my problems as well as how I was suffering from PTSD.

I had my second session a week later and became more at ease with Dr Williamson. He gained my trust, and I allowed myself to properly open up to this man who was helping me so much. Over time, I allowed him to push the boundaries of my traumatised mind. He gave me a better understanding of CBT (cognitive behaviour therapy) and made me have more of an understanding that I was my own therapist and that I had to recognise and understand my own mind, the traumas, and the effects that they were having on my life.

He gave me some homework to start doing each week throughout my course of treatments with him. The homework consisted of two separate sheets of paperwork. One was a daily thought record of positive things that you accomplished each day of your life. The other sheet of paperwork was about the negative thought records of each day, which you must rate as far as how they affect you—from 1 to 100 per cent. It included how it made you feel and what you could do for yourself to change the way you felt to a healthier perspective.

At first, I wondered how this was going to help me, writing about each day of my life and putting positive and negative thoughts into a daily dairy. But over the course of time and all the therapy sessions that I had with Dr Williamson, I would strongly recommend and urge you to do this yourself if you are suffering from PTSD, anxiety, or depression. It truly does help give you a better understanding of your own life and the difficulties that you are struggling with—from your own trauma or another illness that you have encountered with in your life.

The thought records will show you that you are being positive every day of your life, even with things that you would not normally think of too much. As for daily positive thought records, they should have three columns. The first column should be the day and date. The second column should be named 'What I did.' The third one should be named 'Positive personal qualities,' what you have shown or felt.

I went to register with the Helping the Aged charity as a volunteer. Positive personal qualities means being friendly, honest, capable, trustworthy, and kind.

I went to a local college to see about a painting and decorating course to gain my diploma and qualifications in NVQ3 to help me get back into employment. Positive personal qualities means being creative, efficient, and open-minded, showing initiative and being motivated and experienced.

On Wednesday, I went to the gym for the day. I had a good workout, went for a swim, sat in the steam room doing some mind exercises, and then relaxed in the Jacuzzi, chatting to some people I knew.

Positive personal qualities means hard-working, practical, consistent, serious, fit, quick, strong, and supportive.

Take the time to keep a record of your positive actions. It will help while you are suffering from a trauma and struggling to come to terms with how your life has become so different that family and loved ones and close friends tell you that you are not the same person they used to know and once loved. Look at the thought records and tell yourself that you are not losing your mind or cracking up—knowing and recognising your symptoms, you are bound not to be the same person as you were before your trauma. Tell your loved ones to have sympathy, empathy, and show compassion as well as be patient.

I am now going to include some of my own negative thought records. This is an important thing for you to do.

The negative thoughts record sheet is set out in six columns. If you are having therapy or seeing a doctor for PTSD, depression, or another ailment, then you can ask for help in getting some positive thought sheets and negative thought sheets. Each sheet is set out like this. The first column is named 'Situation/Trigger'.

The second column is named 'Emotions/Moods'. Rate from 0 to 100 per cent.

The third column is named 'Physical Sensations'.

The fourth column is named 'Unhelpful Thoughts and Images'.

The fifth column is named 'Alternative Response/Healthier Perspective'.

The sixth column is named 'What I Did/What I Could Do/Diffusion Technique'. Rate between 0 and 100 per cent. My first example is the following:

On Saturday 25 December 2010, my situation trigger was the sight of an ambulance.

'Emotions/Moods': Rate between 0 and 100 per cent.

'Physical Sensations' is being angry, upset, and heart rate soaring, shivers down your spine, standing in a trance-like state and looking at an ambulance.

Unhelpful Thoughts and Images: Returning home from having placed the wreath down at the cemetery, I came across an ambulance with sirens and flashing blue lights. It pulled up alongside me. I was overcome with emotion and anxiety. I stood in a trance-like state and was bombarded with the intrusive image of the sights and sounds of my bike accident. The images were like a child's flip book of pages, with each page being that of my accident which was being flashed before my eyes. I delivered the full events of the accident while standing there, unable to move myself away from this ambulance.

Alternative Response: I managed to drag myself away from the ambulance and walked home, where I did my mindful breathing exercises to calm my nerves at what had just happened, now composed after an hour ago. I drove up for my daughter to bring her to mine for Christmas Day.

On 6 December 2010, I experienced a situation/trigger nightmare: my motions/moods. Rate between 0 and 100 per cent.

Physical Sensations: I woke up screaming and soaked in sweat and had wet the bed again. I was too upset, angry with myself, and frightened to go back to bed.

Unhelpful Thoughts/Image. I woke up screaming. I'd had a nightmare about my accident. I woke at the point where it was laid in a coffin next to my parents, the same usual nightmare I had had at least three to four times in a week.

Alternative Response: I jumped out of bed, changed the sheets, put the wet sheets in the washer, had a bath, took a sleeping tablet, and fell asleep on the settee.

Damian and Dr Williamson helped me get a far greater understanding of my life and the difficulties that I'd had to cope with on my own, with no family to help support me other than Gabrielle. No one else was there for me to help me through the difficult traumas that I had been suffering with for so long. Their help and support was life changing for me. It gave me a more positive outlook of my own life. They helped me regain some of my confidence and made me realise that I had survived all of my traumas and had a lot to offer this world.

My counselling helped me recognise my symptoms and gave me the encouragement to be my own therapist. It showed me ways to use CBT (cognitive behavioural techniques) to recognise when I was having flashbacks, nightmares, and the intrusive ruminating images. It enabled me to recognise the signs and the things that reminded me of all my traumas, also helping me cope far easier than I would have been able to without having a greater understanding of why I suffered with PTSD.

I have had to learn that I am not just suffering from just one trauma but from four, and all of them were in such a short period that I had to accept that most of my problems and difficulties were associated with my bike accident so soon after losing my loved ones.

I have a woman in a silver Ford KA to thank for this, all because she wanted to cut a corner of a junction in order to save time on her short journey.

I have nothing but heartfelt sympathy for any person out there who is trying to cope on their own with the effect of a trauma, no matter what the trauma may have been. It may not have been anything like my four traumas.

Dr Williamson gave me a book called *Overcoming Traumatic Stress*. It inspired me to write my own book to share my traumatic experiences, so it may help inspire sufferers of PTSD to find the help that is out there for PTSD, anxiety, depression, or any other extreme issue. No one has to suffer in silence.

I was pushed to the boundaries of my own existence, and it cost me so much of my life. I have lost relationships over it. I have lost the confidence I once had to be around people socially. I no longer went out because of fears of a panic attack or flashback occurring whilst in crowded places. I no longer work as an asbestos stripper and don a mask daily in case of a flashback or panic attack. I lost friends because of withdrawing myself from society.

It put so many strains and pressures on my life that I am amazed I am not six feet under. It also took away from me something that I will likely never find myself doing again: riding a bicycle. I'd loved doing that since the day my father got me my first bike at the age of 6. My fears and anxieties about ever getting back on a bike and cycling again may be overcome and conquered one day, but I cannot guarantee it. I will have to wait and see.

To summarise how I look at my affliction with PTSD, I would say it put me at the very bottom of a large ladder that is on the inside of a dark well covered in grease. Each time I started climbing the ladder, I kept slipping back to the bottom of the ladder. After the first trauma, I looked up and saw the lost old happy me. I was just looking down into the dark well.

I was broken and trapped in a dark, lonely place filled with eternal pain and sorrow. I would try to climb the ladder, but as I got a rung or two higher, another trauma stopped me in my tracks and prevented me from getting out, knocking me back down the ladder. I found myself trapped. I worried that the happy person I used to be would never be found.

I made one final push for the top of the ladder so I could reclaim my old self and leave the traumatised and battered soul which I had become in the well. I wanted to put a lid on this well and seal it forever. I wanted to reclaim myself again and start living again, to walk the earth in peace and to move on in life.

I never returned to that dark place of hate and anger. I watched myself leave the place of pain, hurt, and sorrow. I left my traumatised soul behind and eventually reached the top. I had suffered enough. I was now filled with hope as I emerged. The sunlight struck through a shimmer of clouds as I raised the lid over the well, sealing it forever. I walked away from this well with a slight breeze drafting against the reclaimed Daniel Osborne. I took a long hard look in a mirror and saw something that I had not seen in many years. I saw a man looking back at me with a glimmer of a smile. This filled my heart with emotion, not of pain this time but of hope and peace. He was a person I had not seen or recognised in such a long time. He was a man who now had the power to start living again. It was the lost me, the person I was who felt years of pain and traumas, bereavements, and near loss of life. And so the journey began.

It was a challenge, but I made positive small steps to push myself, to make my daughter proud of me. I am now alive again with a smile and a future that I could be in control of.

Do not give in to the traumas that are damaging your life. There is a light at the end of the tunnel. There are means and ways to seek help in order to guide you on your own journey of life, but you have to be one hundred per cent committed to putting some hard work into yourself. You will learn to become your own therapist, and you will become a greater person because of all your efforts and hard work.

Over the course of time, and with the help of keeping positive and negative daily thought records, you will eventually confront your traumas head-on, learning to accept that you are not losing your mind and that you are normal. As each day passes and you read the positive daily thought records, you will realise that you do many good and positive things every day without realising you have done them. Of course, you will find, as I did, that it is very strange to write these down. You may think it's a waste of, but trust me that it isn't. Just writing your thoughts down is a positive step to start with.

Write down all the upsetting things, the difficult things, the ones that are making your daily life a traumatic place to live. Feel free to write down all the terrifying things that you don't want to share or talk about. If you stick to your guns and write these down, you will find that you're in a better position in your life than I was.

You may have a wife, husband, mother, father, brothers, sisters, or close friends to show you true support. Let these loved ones see your positive and negative thought records, allowing them to have a bigger understanding of what you are going through each day and how you truly feel. This will help them understand why you are feeling the way you are and make them aware that you are still you. Don't let them say negative things to you, that you're not the same person you used to be. Tell them you have not gone anywhere, that you are still there but need the time and support from each of them. It will help you enormously to know that they are giving you positive support and love. Help them understand it and you will have far more than I ever had. Yet I'm still here battling on and am a far more positive person for it.

I strongly recommend reading *Overcoming Traumatic Stress,* a self-help guide to cognitive techniques. This good book will give you an understanding of PTSD and ways in which you can help become your own therapist. If you have use of the internet, I advise doing a search to find all the loads of free information on PTSD. You will also find the positive and negative thought sheets that you can download and use. You will find information and stories of other people's traumas, which will help you understand your own trauma.

Consult with your doctor about how you feel and ask to be referred to a therapist, counsellor, or a similar organisation, as they are out there to help you. Otherwise, you may well suffer in silence, which I wouldn't want you to do. There is also a disc which you can download or buy called the wellbeing relaxation cd. It has four good exercises on it for you: mindfulness of breath and body; mindfulness of sounds, thoughts, and emotions; breathing space; and loving kindness meditation. If you have difficulty finding this disc, ask your doctor or therapist to see if they can help you find it.

Seek out the help that is out there; it will help you more than you could imagine. But be open-minded and prepared to put the hard work in yourself, as if you don't, you won't move forward and will remain stuck and suffering on your own in silence. It's better to overcome your trauma and learn to cope with life with PTSD. It will make you become a stronger person at the end of your own journey of life. Don't give up.

Unfortunately, it was not the end of the road, and I was forced to continue my journey yet again with another trauma, the loss of a true friend, my best mate, Stan the man.

CHAPTER 5

TRAUMA 5

The passing of my best friend
Stan the Man, 43 years of age 1968-2011

Bad news was to take hold of me once more. Another trauma consumed my life just after I thought my life was about to start with fresh meaning and purpose. So much has happened. I moved from my old flat into my new one to begin a fresh start, a new beginning, which I was so excited about. I felt for the first time that maybe something good was going to progress from this move, maybe find a positive frame of mind to help me live a normal life and move a step closer to finding some peace.

But after only being in my new home for ten days, I found that bad news was to follow me once more. Upon returning home one day from the gym in a good frame of mind, happy and slowly moving on with life, I received a phone call which would shatter me and completely destroy my soul once more, completely turning my world upside down. A friend named Jacob rang me, and I instantly wondered why he was phoning me. He never did. 'Jacob, what can I do for you?' I asked.

'Daniel, I have some bad news for you. Have you heard about Stan?'

I said I hadn't and asked what was up with Stan. He gave me the news that Stan was on his way home last night and that he had sadly passed away. At first, I thought it was some kind of sick joke, as Stan was only 43 years old and was a fit and healthy man. What Jacob was telling me made no sense, and my emotions ran wild. 'What are you on about? Stan's not dead. Where did you hear this?'

He gave me the only information he knew himself as far as what he had heard. He said that Stan had been out for drinks with my old friends who wanted nothing to do with me, and they went to my old friend's house to continue having drinks. His partner had called him about 1.30 a.m. to see where he was and ask him when he would be home. He'd replied that he'd be home soon and that he didn't feel very well. Jacob said he'd heard that Stan had slipped away from the gathering to go home. He'd only gotten 150 yards away from his friend's house and was later found collapsed. A passer-by called for the police and an ambulance, but they were apparently too late. Stan did not make it home to his family, and he is no longer with us, sadly.

I burst into tears and threw up, trying to make sense of what I had just heard. After the devastating news about my good friend Stan, I tried to compose myself. I was dazed and confused, questioning whether what I had just been told could be true. Was he truly gone? How could this be?

I drove to another friend's house around the corner. I pulled up and knocked on my friend James's door, but it was his brother Aron who answered the door. I went in and began to break down. Aron said, 'What's up, Daniel? Are you OK?'

I told him I wasn't OK and asked where James was, saying that I needed to tell him something. He said James was in bed, so I went upstairs and yelled at him to get up and come downstairs, which he did. He sat with Aron in their front room, and I told them both about the phone call I had just received. I could see by their eyes that they didn't believe me. They started questioning whether it could be true.

I looked at them both with tear-filled eyes and told them it was true, that he had passed away last night. I said that I was not exactly sure what happened, that I only knew what Jacob had told me. If it weren't for Jacob phoning me, I would not have known, as none of the friends Stan was with on that night would have thought to let me know about my best friend. They were the same mates who had fallen out with me, as I mentioned earlier in this book.

I told James and Aron about Stan. They made a phone call to their other brother, who was Aron's twin, Terrence, a close friend of Stan's. He broke down in tears over the phone as I had when I'd found out. I remember going home to my new flat and sobbing for hours, trying to come to terms with the devastating news. I called Gabrielle for support, and she came down to stay with me.

We later went to pay our respects to Stan's beloved family. I was totally overcome with emotions and recall just holding them all as we sobbed uncontrollably in each others' arms. I was speechless, lost for words of comfort for them. I knew from losing my parents and auntie that nothing I or anyone else said at that time would make any comfort to Stan' partner and her two girls.

I knew what lay ahead for them all, and I offered my support and love as best I could, leaving them all to comfort and console one another.

I returned home to my new flat with my daughter, and she comforted until I nearly passed out from mental exhaustion.

Later that same night, I received a phone call from James, Aron's brother, who was now proper drunk with drink. He was chewing my ear off with profanities. I ended the phone call and drifted off to sleep again on my sofa. I then suddenly woke up and told my daughter I had just had the strangest of dreams, that James had just rung me, having a go at me.

Gabrielle looked at me and said, 'You weren't dreaming, Dad. He just rang you.'

I instantly became enraged with disgust that he could have done such a thing, especially after what we had all just learnt about losing our mate Stan. I called him straight back and had a right go at him, but truthfully I think it was a waste of time, as he was so drunk. I could hear a houseful of people shouting at James to stop going on. Going to bed was all I wanted to do at this point.

James and Aron along with the other brother, Terrence, had been lifelong mates, but I have not really spoken to James because of what he said to me that night. One day I suppose I'll amend the friendship in some ways—but only when it feels right to do so.

A few days after I was told of my friend Stan, I spoke with his partner, Laura, in regards to wanting to visit Stan at the funeral parlour to pay my respects and to say my final goodbyes to a true and genuinely remarkable man. She said she would contact me and make arrangements for me to go there, which she did a day or two later.

So I arrange to meet my friend who'd cared for my auntie Meredith at the funeral parlour, as she also wanted to pay her respects. She knew Stan through me when we used to date one another, and I needed the support of her. The prospect of having to visit another funeral home so shortly after my parents and auntie died scared the daylights out of me. We met up and ended up going in together. As were going in, I met Gaby and Sophia, Stan's daughters, who were just coming out. I consoled both Gaby & Sophia and told them how devastated we all were. They told me that there mam Laura was in there, along with Stan's sister Jacquelyn.

We all held each other and cried, trying to comfort each other. My attention then focused on my dear friend Stan lying there and looking peaceful. In some strange way, it brought a tearful smile to my face. I said to Laura that he looked as if he were ready to go to Glastonbury or camping. He wasn't wearing a suit, just his beloved Ron Hill trousers and a camping shirt, which was somewhat appropriate and befitting.

Laura said that she thought so too, as this was how we all loved and remembered him Daniel. She held me close, and we cried together. Then she and Stan's sister Jacquelyn asked me if I'd like to be alone with him to say my goodbyes to him. I said yes, and they both left the room.

I told him I'd love him forever and would think of him for the rest of my days. 'You are the most amazing person and friend that I have ever had come into my life, and I will always be there to support your family and do right by them if they ever need me. I love you, mukka.' I kissed him a fond farewell and did my best to comfort his family upon leaving.

Stan's funeral was packed. He was that loved and so well thought of that half of the area must have been there paying their respects and saying goodbye to Stan.

After the funeral at the crematorium, there was a wake held for Stan in a local social club, but I did not attend, unfortunately. I feared that if I were to turn up there and pay my respects, it would be too uncomfortable for me, especially because people who used to be my friends would be there. I thought there would be some animosity towards me. They were the same bunch of lads I had not seen or spoken to in such a long time. I did explain this to Stan's family beforehand, so they understood my reasons for not going. They assured me it was OK, but I do regret not going. I just didn't want to be the cause of anything. It simply did not feel appropriate. I hoped Stan would look down at me and forgive me. I am sorry, my good friend.

Goodbye, Stan. You were one of the nicest and fun-loving people I have ever come across. I will miss our friendship forever, my mate. May you rest in peace. You have left a legacy behind you, Stan, that will stay in our hearts forever. You truly were special and one in a million, a truly remarkable guy.

RIP, mukka. You were my best friend. I still have all the memories of the adventures we had together, from our time going to the lakes to all the camping we did. I will never forget the time we went up to the hills and you let me set off a distress flare. I remember that it lit up the whole of our area. I remember you holding me with sheer excitement. I think half the population saw it also.

I remember our times at Glastonbury. The first year we went, I think it was 1998. It was a mudfest, and we were knee deep in mud. You'd shown up in shorts and trainers. We danced to James live singing 'Sit Down.'

We also caught Faithless, and you and I danced until the early hours with bin liners for trousers and just our trainers on. And even the brass plague that we cemented in our camping tunnel this was a place from were me and Stan along with other friends used to go camping and It was a reservoir and on one side of it was a hollow cement tunnel that we had made a lot memories there we used a snow Sledge once to slide down the inside of the tunnel we had such fun there that myself and Stan went up one day and placed a brass plaque with all our names on it on the inside of the tunnel were it still stands to this day we placed it there in the sept 97 . These memories will stay with me throughout my entire life, and I will light a candle for you each evening alongside the ones I light for my mam, dad, and auntie. I will miss you forever. Love, as always.

So that was yet another trauma I had to cope with. I started to ask myself the question once again if anything else bad could happen. 'Please, God, let there be a change in my life,' I prayed. 'Let something good happen to me.'

I think he truly heard my voice. As the final chapter of my journey unfolds, I am blessed with wondrous love and happiness, which brought the journey to a pleasant ending. Long may my journey of hope and peace continue.

Things have really begun to change in my life after all the turmoil's and traumas that I had to endure, mostly on my own and with Gabrielle. Things moved on so quickly and I have now settled into my new home that I have now managed to buy. I have a beautiful place to live and can now say I have found peace I have a place where I can finally begin to live a normal life, a life without the stress and the worries of thinking is something bad going to happen to me as I have done for so many years of my difficult past life.

My life has come full circle now, a miraculous turnaround. I have found peace and a positive state of mind away from all the negative things that had surrounded my life for so many years. The traumas of late seemed to be slowly fading into the shadows, and I found myself almost at the very top of my ladder that I spoke about. I am now so close to stepping off that final rung of my ladder and reclaiming the lost me back from the abyss of my traumatised life. I have found the lost me, the person I once was before all the difficulties of what my own journey took me through. I am now a far greater person, a more confident person. I overcame so many difficulties with Gabrielle's support. The life I now seek for myself is the life of a normal human being where I can begin to bloom and flourish.

To start this positive part of my journey, I'll go back to January 2012. It began with the news that my beautiful daughter had found someone she was so besotted with, a lovely guy by the name of Stu. She quickly fell head over heels in love with him, and after a short while, she moved away from the family nest and set up a home with Stu down south in Pontefract, where they began their lives together. After a few months, my daughter called me to give me the first good news, the first in over ten years. She said, 'Hi, Dad. I've got something to tell you!'

'Go on then. Is everything OK?' I asked.

She said that everything was fine. 'Stu has asked me to marry him, and I said yes.'

I was lost for words at first. Then I said, 'Oh my God, that is great news, darling. I am so pleased for you. I bet you are buzzing.'

'Yes, Dad, I am! I'm so pleased that you are OK with it.'

'You're my daughter, and I only want to see you happy in life. You have lived through so much in your young life and witnessed so much that I only want to see you happy and enjoy life to the fullest.'

'I *am* happy, Dad,' she said.

From that moment on, my life began to open up. I began to start living my life again. I had been brought back from a dark place to the land of the living. A switch had been ignited within me, and it began to burn brighter and brighter every day.

After the wonderful news of my daughter getting engaged, I began to look forward to the next bit of good news that might come into my life. Sure enough it came up shortly after that. Yet again it came from my daughter. She told me that there was going to be an addition to the Osborne family. She was pregnant. I was totally blown away by this. 'Oh, my darling daughter!' I exclaimed.

She was no longer my little princess. She was now on her own two feet in life, living her life to the fullest and expecting her first child, my first grandson. I was once again blown away with the news. I'd been shocked at first, but once the news sunk in, I filled up with the joy of becoming a granddad. It was as if my heart had been charged with a booster from God himself. I could feel the positive flow of life running through my veins. The worn-out traumatised tired veins were being filled up and replaced with a charge of positive energy. I congratulated my daughter and future son-in-law, Stu, on their news. I told them how proud I was and told them I loved them both.

So now with the joy of becoming a granddad in 2013 it felt like the turning point for me. I continued to work and keep busy during the year. I made close friends with people I had not seen in a few years, and their friendships have helped me in many ways. Because of that, I became a stronger person in life in so many different ways, and for this I cannot thank them enough.

The first of these friendships that I owe gratitude for is my friend Vanessa. Over the last several years or more, she has helped me hold things together when things became too tough to handle. She helped me during times when I had bad spells of back pain, unable to walk or get up from the sofa for weeks at a time, even if just being there to chat things over with, just to be there and listen when no one else could, although she was overcoming certain difficulties in her own life, which I have helped her with. I think that in many ways we helped each other overcome difficulties, and we still remain very good friends. We have slowly moved on and found a purpose once more in our own lives. She has now settled down with a nice guy and is happy in life. I am so pleased for her.

Now to the second person that I owe many thanks to. Once again, it was a friendship that was once there before in my life, but we became distant and had never really seen each other for a long time until I moved into my new home and found she only lived across the road from me, a wonderful person called Carla and her two children, Dominic and Isabella. We began to talk and became friends after a few months of my starting a new life in my new home.

We started talking one day and asked each other how things had been since we had last spoken or seen one another. I found that she had had another child since I last saw here, a beautiful daughter named Isabella. I congratulated her. Dominic, her son, is now ten years old, and I barely recognised him. The last time I had seen him he was only five or six. I remembered thinking how quickly the years had gone by since last seeing them.

It was so nice to see her doing well and having another child. I said that I was glad that we had spoken to one another and that if she ever wanted a chat or a cuppa to call over to my new flat and that she was welcome any time. From that day on, we have been very good friends. I found out as our friendship grew over the course of time just how much of a valued friend she was to become.

To start with, I have to say that I have never come across someone with such a positive outlook on life. Carla has such a positive aura about her that her influence, her outlook and attitude, have rubbed off on me. She has truly helped me become far more focused in my own life and my own goals and achievements.

A breath of fresh air was now warming my heart, and I began to start living a more peaceful life, the life that I had been longing for for so many years. It was now beginning to take shape. The reclaimed me from the top of my ladder was finally starting to walk amongst the land of the living once more.

Carla recommended a book that she said would be good for me: *The Secret,* by Rhonda Byrne. I instantly went out and bought a copy of. All I can say is that if you have not read this book yet, buy it. I found it very helpful. It helps you to appreciate the life that we are given and to live it to the fullest. It helps you focus on becoming positive-minded and focus on life in a way that I never made sense of until reading it.

So I have now had my life in order with a purpose and some goals to achieve. I am truly thankful for every day that I wake up, and I make every day full of positives and wonderful things, letting go of all the negative things in my life that had been dragging me down for so long.

Carla, Dominic, and Isabella have all played a huge part in my life and continue to support me and be there for me when I need it. I genuinely believe that the difficulties that I faced most of my life in the passing of my family and friends—all the traumas and bad luck that pushed my life to the bottom of my ladder and which had become the only things I had known and was accustomed to— are now behind me. All the traumas which I have gone through in my journey of life have pushed and tested my beliefs to the very limits. It was a journey that I nearly gave up on many times, but with the help of all the people that I have spoken of in this book, I have managed to survive my journey and have come out of it a more confident and positive human with a far greater respect of the life that I have been given.

My daughter and her partner moved from Pontefract to be closer to her mother and sister as well as myself. They settled into their new home. With Christmas drawing near, for the first time in years I began to feel that I didn't want to shut myself away and hide from Christmas as I had for many years since losing all my family. I even put up a small Christmas tree in my flat with a few decorations, something that I hadn't done for as long as I could remember. This was the start of a healthier, happier life.

Christmas was now here, and Gabrielle and Stu invited me for Christmas lunch, which I gladly accepted. I was blown away with it what a magnificent time I had with my daughter and her partner I tell Stu that he is in the long line of work because let me tell you the guy has got talents in a kitchen it was by far the best Christmas lunch and best Christmas I have had in many years.

The year of 2012 saw me get my home and a nice new car. The wonderful news of my daughter getting engaged and the prospects of becoming a granddad were truly a massive turnaround. If you have managed to join me in getting this far into my journey, I thank you for sharing my journey with me. It was an extremely difficult thing to write this book. It is not something that I thought I would ever foresee, my putting my thoughts and feelings on paper. That in itself is a massive positive achievement for me. My story is about showing people that yes, we go through some really horrific traumas. We are sometimes pushed to the edge of life. We get our lives driven into a place of no return.

The mind gets punished as it gets pulled deeper and deeper into a negative state of mind. We as humans accept this and feel as if it's normal simply because our minds get used to it. We get used to being traumatised. It causes us to soak up all the negative unwanted energies that fill our lives instead of all the good and positive energy that can fill our lives.

So do not give up hope if you have suffered a traumatic experience or have lost loved ones and you feel that there is no hope left for you, as there is always hope for us all. If it means that it takes you on your own journey of life, then once you begin, you will come out a far more positive person who will truly live a peaceful happy life, leaving all the traumas and bad things behind you forever.

January 2013 started with the arrival of my grandson Ethan, a healthy, beautiful child. It was a whole new chapter to look forward to. My life had come full circle with him being born. It gave me the boost to carry things forward for the future, a future that is to be filled with nothing other than positivity and no more negativity for me. I have looked back at my life and all the traumas and extreme difficulties that I had to face, which has pushed me mentally and physically. It has made me question my beliefs and thoughts. It has broken me, but with the right kind of help and support, whether it be doctors, counsellors, my daughter, or close friends who have stood by me and not given up on me, they have all played a massive part in my life. Without these people, I would have lost hope long ago.

I was now at the end of my journey of life with PTSD though I don't think it will ever leave me for good, and life was looking good. I am currently pursuing various options that lie ahead of me, and for once I can say that I feel excited about facing the future. I am no longer stuck and at the bottom of my ladder. I have found my way to the top and love the person I have now become.

My final thoughts are that we are only human. The mind is a powerful thing. If we allow our minds to get pulled into a negative state, whether it be from a trauma or something else, it allows our minds to become a magnet for attracting more and more of the same kind. We will continue to attract negative thoughts, feelings, and emotions. It's extremely hard for this cycle to change, no matter what we do. Once this takes hold of us, it will break us down and pull our lives apart. It can destroy relationships with family and friends, as they will not fully understand the complexity of the state of your mind and how broken-hearted and alone you feel. This is how it was for me for so many years of my life, but my life may be different from your own. You may have a closer relationship with your brothers and sisters than what I have had. With family and friends behind you, you will pull through things far better than I did, as I never had that help. I only had my daughter, Gabrielle, and lots of therapists, doctors, and counsellors.

If you have their love and support, you will pull through things far better than the way I have managed to do. I no doubt would have managed a lot better with all of the traumas that I have had to face mostly alone.

Do not lose hope and do not give in. Don't let your traumas defeat you, as you are not alone. Seek professional help if you need it; do not suffer in silence and alone. If you do, your soul will get dragged away from you, which makes trauma even harder to overcome.

If my book gives just one person the courage to fight and to turn their life around, then all the time and effort, the tears and turmoil, will have been worthwhile for me.

This has to have been one of the most difficult stories I ever had to write. It is also my first attempt at writing a book, and I hope that you take something out of the journey that I have had to go through, all the pain and suffering. If it makes sense to you as you finish my journey, then I truly hope it gives you the courage to seek the help you need. Do not stay traumatised and suffer in silence as I have had to for many years. Get help and start the process of overcoming your own fears. Face your traumas head-on, and if you have to have therapy to help you, then do it. Don't think that you are a weak person for accepting their help. It helped me and gave me the strength to climb my ladder to reclaim the lost me.

Over the last twenty years, I have picked this book up with the hopes of eventually getting it published in order to help people, and now that I am making the decision to do so and am finalising it and getting it ready for publication, I thought it would be appropriate to add a few further things which are extremely high positives. I feel that it will give an overall perspective of where my life currently is after all the traumas that fell before me. I knew I had to overcome a few of my fears and phobias and try to lay them to rest.

I managed to overcome my fear of hospitals and everything that I associated with them, the sights, the sounds, the smells, the blue lights, and the faces that I had become so familiar with. I managed this by undertaking four days of work inside the hospital that had taken so much from me. I did the four days of work and used it as self-therapy.

I was employed to repaint the orthodontics department, which gave me the opportunity to walk the wards and corridors I had spent so much time in with my traumas. It allowed me to put them to rest and enabled me to further move on with my life. It was difficult to do this, but it actually worked for me. It rid me of my phobias.

Upon completing the painting of the orthodontics department, the company that employed me to do the work was taken with me and with my standards of work. They asked me to continue working in the hospital where I had lost so much. I had a meeting with the head manager, an amazing guy called Tony. I explained to him why I took on the four days of work, that it was to put a few ghosts, fears, and phobias to rest. Tony said he wanted me to continue to work there and said that if I would consider doing so, he and the company would support me throughout my time there. Filled with positivity and confidence, I took on the job. I spent nearly seven years working in the hospital that took so much from me. I am so glad that I did, as it helped me become a lot more positive and confident. It also helped shake off the fears that I had held on to for so long.

My daughter has continued in her life and now has four boys, so I am a granddad to four amazing, cheeky little minions, or monkeys, as I like to refer to them. They are living happily down south, closer to her husband's side of the family.

My son has recently had a child also, which made me a grandad again. But with the year now being 2020 and with the pandemic sweeping across the globe, I have not yet seen my grandson George. But I am excited and can't wait to do so. I found an amazing full-time job with a company that has to be the best company I have ever worked for. I underwent and completed a mental health first aid course through my company. I passed it successfully and am loving every second of it.

I am now finalising my book and have an author ID (massive accomplishment) and a publication company that is fully backing and helping me. I commissioned a well-known local artist to design the image for my book. May my journey continue in the positive way it is. I hope that there is an end in sight to this COVID-19 pandemic that is destroying so many lives around the globe.

I would like to thank everyone who has helped me in writing this book. Who knows—I may return to writing about a more pleasant and happier journey in the near future.

I hope that after reading my book you have gotten a little bit of encouragement from it. I would like to thank you for taking the time to read about my journey. I truly hope you enjoyed it.

Keep safe and well. Help promote empathy and encouragement around the world. Let's not judge people and instead learn to look at humankind in a non judgemental way show compassion and love to one another.

As you never know what is hidden under a smile a smile can hide a thousand pains and sorrows. I know mine did.

Best wishes on your own life's journey.
Keep safe during these difficult covid times and look out for one another always smile and stay positive through life's journey and what it has to offer remember this is not the end nor is it the beginning or the beginning of the end just the end of the beginning.

We are only here on this wonderful earth to live our lives once so embrace every moment of every day and cherish everyone in your life.

Daniel Osborne.

ABOUT THE AUTHOR

The Journey of my self taken on a path that would lead me to the lowest depths in my life a place that I could not have possibly ever forseen a journey that destroyed my soul. But a journey that pushed the human mind to some where that a man need not wish to ever take alone and to come out of it a better person full of life and positivity focused motivated and living life and not taking it for granted.

Printed in the United States
by Baker & Taylor Publisher Services